Cure for the Incurable

—+—

Your Physical Healing in the Lord Jesus Christ

By Greg S. Pettys

XULON PRESS

Acknowledgments

—+—

S pecial thanks to my awesome wife, Johnita, who exemplifies Proverbs 31. Her faith in Jesus Christ our Healer has helped me to keep spreading this message both through our children Daniel, Kara Joy, James, Alicia, Kyle, and Blake and to many in other places throughout the world.

It is with great respect and gratitude that I acknowledge the foundations laid in this topic by the preaching and writings of such great believing practitioners of Divine Healing as Justin Martyr, Ireneus, Origen, Clement, Augustine, Martin Luther, Zenzendorf, the Waldensies, John Wesley, Peter Cartright, A.J. Gordon, John Alexander Dowie, A.B. Simpson, John G. Lake, Amy Semple McPhearson, Smith Wigglesworth, Oral Roberts, Kathryn Kuhlman, William Branum, E.W. Kenyon, W.V. Grant, Jack Coe, Derek Prince, T. L. Osborn, John, Dodie, and son Joel Osteen, Kenneth E. Hagin, and son Kenneth Hagin, Jr., Kenneth and Gloria Copeland, Dr. Lester Sumrall, Benny Hinn, Dr. John F. Avanzini, and my own dear friend Don Blevins.

The editing help of both Evelyn Schumacher and my daughter, Alicia Pettys was indispensable. Thanks to Phil Bradshaw of Image Chamber for the special cover art work and graphics on the Indian translations of this book.

I am deeply grateful for my growing partnerships with all of my dear Indian brothers including Moses Navgire, Joshua

Motiwar, Nana Dar, Y. M. Dupte, David Sarkar, Thomas Yohannan, Benjamin Wadekar, and Dr. Jacob Tony.

Finally, hats off to all the fine people at my publisher, XULON Press, who made my second book experience even more enjoyable than the first.

To all those who have been told
they have incurable ailments,
sicknesses, and diseases.
May this book be used by Jesus
Christ the Great Physician to bring
you healing, health, and
a long life of serving the Master.

Table of Contents

———+———

Forward

---+---

J esus is the Healer for all mankind's need today. No man can claim to be a healer for in truth only God can heal. All healing methods including the best medical science has to offer are at best merely assisting God's healing process. Those of us who are instruments of the Spirit of God's supernatural healing power are called by some today "faith healers". The title is sometimes used in derision or unbelieving ridicule. My position on this title "faith healer" is as the apostle Peter explained in Acts chapter 3 after the healing of the lame man at the Gate Beautiful. He explained, "His Name (Jesus), through faith in His Name has made this man strong." So in the sense that God does heal through our faith in His Mighty Name then we are in truth "faith healers.'

Recently I was in an audience where someone taught that modern "faith healers" are not healing organic sicknesses as much as dealing with functional symptoms, pathological alteration, or psychiatric disorders. I was deeply moved to set forth in these pages both the Word of God on Divine Healing and the plethora of human experiences today that are in line with these Scriptures and prove otherwise. The speaker's argument was that if God is still in the divine healing and miracle business then "let us see the restoration of organs, re-growth of limbs, the opening of blind eyes, and raising of the dead like in Jesus' day." Well then may this book be the clear testimony of just what he was looking for!

The first of many great examples I hope to set forth that God still is healing the incurable kinds of ailments is the healing of Evelyn Schumacher, one of the editors of this book. The following is her story:

At age 65 I had a routine colonoscopy that revealed a large polyp requiring surgery. Several feet of my intestine were removed. Early tests showed no cancer but that would not be confirmed until after surgery was completed.

At the time I received this news, my employer, Dr. Mark Wood was hosting the author of this book, teaching a seminar on Divine Healing. I attended some of the meetings before I had surgery. I began listening to tapes on healing, reading books and praying healing scriptures over myself.

Surgery went well. During a deep sleep, in my spirit, I could see healing activity going on in the colon area. I knew that a supernatural healing was taking place.

My hospital stay was brief (4 days), I was back to work part time in 2 weeks after surgery, and full time in 3 ½ weeks.

In my opinion, God healed me supernaturally and also by the use of traditional medicine. I believe that getting the "Word of God" into my mind, spirit and body is what made the difference in the speed and the ease of my recovery.

Reading this book can change your life and the truths contained can cure the incurable!

~Evelyn Schumacher

Introduction

—+—

When Jesus spoke so often of the "Gospel of the Kingdom", it always included the healing of all sickness, all diseases, and the releasing of people who believed Jesus from all their torments.

· **Matthew 4:23-24** says, "And Jesus went about all Galilee, teaching in their synagogues, preaching **the Gospel of the Kingdom, and healing all manner of sickness, and all manner of disease among the people.** And his fame went throughout all Syria, and they brought to him all sick people that were taken with diverse diseases, and torments, and those which were possessed with devils, and those which were lunatic, and those who had the palsy, **and he healed them.**"

· In **Matthew 10**, we see Jesus speak of this same gospel when He commissioned his disciples, saying, "As you go, preach, saying, **"The Kingdom of Heaven is at hand. Heal the sick, cleanse the lepers, raise the dead, and cast out demons."** So, we see that everywhere that Jesus is he preaches his gospel; in that is healing of the body, deliverance of the spirit, and freedom of the mind.

· The next scripture is **Mark 16: 15-20**, which is known as the Great Commission. It is as follows: "Jesus said unto them, **'Go ye unto all the world and preach the gospel** to every creature. He that believeth and is baptized shall be saved. But he that believeth not shall be damned. And these signs shall follow them that believe: In my name, you will cast out devils, speak with new tongues, take up serpents, and if you drink of any deadly thing, it will not harm you. **You shall lay hands on the sick, and they shall recover.'** So then, after the Lord had spoken unto then, he was received up into Heaven, sitting at the right hand of God."

Literally, the Greek word for believe means "the believing ones." That includes all of us. Notice, he didn't say it will follow the apostles of the first century, the apostles, or the prophets. He said all who believe, and that is us.

· Let us now look at **John 14:12-14**. **"Verily, verily, (or truly, truly) I say to you, he that believeth in me, the works that I do shall he do also, (and this is what's coming in these days) and greater works than these shall he do,** because I go to my Father; and whatever any of you asks in my name, that will I do, that the Father may be glorified in the Son."

Is healing part of the "anything" Jesus spoke of here? Yes!! Are we believers? Yes!! Then we can do things even greater than Christ, because He's gone away and sent the power of his Holy Spirit to us, the body of believers. God's got an army, and we're marching through the land. Deliverance is our cry, and there's healing in our hand. The reason we can do the greater works is not because they are greater than what he did in magnitude; instead, they are greater in multitude, for there are a billion followers of Christ. We are the hands that lay on the sick, and Christ can do greater works through those who believe. So why don't the greater works occur? Why aren't there healings today, in this age of rapid medical advancements, biotechnology, cloning, DNA research, and expansion of exploratory drugs? Many people are suffering and dying needlessly from what are considered "incurable" sicknesses and diseases because they do not know what the Word of God says about Divine Healing. I estimate that in prayer meetings that I have attended over the last 30 years that seven out of every ten prayer requests are for physical needs. Yet, as the prophet said in **Hosea 4:6, "My people are destroyed for lack of knowledge."**

In absorbing the Biblical truth in this book, we are going to watch God build faith for healing and health in your hearts, brothers and sisters. Moreover, many of you will be used to turn the course of households, communities, churches, and even entire nations because of this Divine Healing Book!

Chapter One-
Approaching the Healer

—+—

J esus is the Healer. We read in the Bible true stories that
show both the right and wrong way to approach our Healer,
Jesus. In **Luke 7:36 – 50**, we read about a woman who the
passage says was sinful, implying that she was probably a
prostitute. This prostitute heard about the Lord's goodness,
kindness, and mercy, and she knew she needed his cleansing
and forgiveness. She found out that our Lord was invited into
the home of a Pharisee for dinner, and so she went there. Jesus
was reclined, leaning on one elbow as the Old Testament
saints would do, when the sinful woman came quietly into
the room and stood behind Jesus. The woman wouldn't even
come into the presence of the Lord without standing humbly
behind him, for she was convicted of her sins.

So, we see that true worship came from the humble heart
this woman had in the presence of the Lord. She began to cry
as she was repenting of her sins, her tears falling on Jesus'
feet. But, as she cried in conviction about her current state,
the Pharisee thought to himself how disgusting this sinner
woman was!

Then, she knelt down to wipe the Holy One's feet with
her hair. This put her down in a position of complete humility
before the Lord, crying over her wretched state. This is a

beautiful form of worship, because she went on to kiss his feet. In **Psalms 2** it says we too should "kiss the son lest he be angry with thee." So, she was practicing faith in Jesus' power to remove her soul's sinful stains.

She then took something out of her life that she had treasured for all her adult years- her life savings, which she kept in an alabaster jar. A jar full of alabaster ointment was very expensive, and would have been very precious to this woman. Perhaps it was to be sold at some future time for financial security, like we would save up a nest egg for our retirement fund. The sinner woman opened up the bottle, and poured out her very life and her future security. Yes, she poured it out on the Lord's feet, filling the room with a sweet aroma.

While our Lord was watching, the Pharisee was still thinking critically of the situation, for he thought that if this man were truly a prophet, he would know that she's a sinner and stop her! To the religious hypocrite, the fact that Jesus did not stop the woman from pouring her alabaster jar out on his feet confirmed that he wasn't of God. Here the sinner woman was worshipping the Lord as her new found God. In contrast the religious man who supposedly represented God to the people of his day was wondering if Jesus was even a prophet. He was the acceptable religious leader while she was a scorned sinner in the community.

The Lord looked at the woman, and then asked the Pharisee, "Simon, see this woman?" He replied, "Yes master." This religious man probably assumed that Jesus was going to rebuke the sinner for her outlandish act; instead, Jesus said something that stunned the Pharisee. He pointed out the difference in how the woman and Simon had treated him- while the woman had wet his feet with her tears, Simon didn't give Jesus, a guest in his home, any water for his feet or ointment for his head. Perhaps Jesus challenged him with something like, "Didn't you know you're supposed to do that Simon? You're supposed to wash my feet and anoint my head? This woman poured out her valuable perfume on his feet, but nothing but doubt had poured out from the Pharisee.

Then Jesus told him a powerful story that ties into how those in need of healing today should approach the Healer. He said that there were two people who owed the bank a lot of money. One of them owed five hundred pence or *denare*, which is one piece of silver, and at that time was worth about one day's wages. The other man another owed only fifty. The money lender forgave them both, because neither could repay their debts. Jesus went on to ask Simon which of these debtors loves the money lender the most? Simon said he assumed it would be the one who had the most forgiven.

Jesus confirmed that this answer was correct, and then finished with one of the most powerful lessons on grace in the Bible. He said that this woman, whose sins were many, loved him much. He let the truth sink in- worship is from a heart of love, and Simon the Pharisee didn't love the Lord. He was only doing his religious duty.

So, we need to ask ourselves if we are approaching God for healing for the right reason. Is it just what we feel that we should do out of duty, or are we approaching the Healer in order to pour out our alabaster ointment? Is approaching God when in a time of need something that many of us were trained to do since we were little children, or are we approaching the Healer in order to pour out our alabaster ointment? Is approaching God to ask for help merely to make us feel better, or are we approaching the Healer in order to pour out our alabaster ointment? Are we known as Christians based upon the attendance records of a church, or are we approaching the Healer in order to pour out our alabaster ointment? Do we go through the motions of attending services or going through other ordinances and liturgy in the church just because it is expected of us, or are we approaching the Healer in order to pour out our alabaster ointment?

There is something precious from our hearts that we should give the Lord, who as the Healer is esteemed to be worthy of our most precious gifts! Our alabaster jar of ointment is when we bring Jesus the Healer the full range of our worshipful expression from the heart! Let us pour out all of our emotions with sincere devotion.

In **Psalms 47:1** it says that we, all God's people, should clap our hands and shout to the Lord with a voice of victory! In fact, **Psalms 150** says for us to praise the Lord, both in the sanctuary and out in the magnitude of his expansive outdoors! It goes on to say for us to praise the Lord with crashing loud cymbals, as well as with stringed instruments, flutes, trumpets, tambourines, and even a little dance! Yes, we can even dance in the Holy Spirit's anointing, just as King David's heart, which was like God's, danced before the Lord. He danced with such exuberance that his wife said "you're making a fool out of yourself." King David's reply to her request for him to stop dancing in front of all the dignified people of Israel was that if she thought that this dancing stuff was foolish, then he would dance even more!

On the other hand, we can also be still and know that Jesus truly is in control of our situation with calm, quiet confidence. "The Lord is in his holy temple: let all the earth keep silence before him," states God in **Habakkuk 2:20.** Yes, we should enjoy being still and silent before him and just know that he is God. So, whether it's complete silence and reverence before our Lord, or whether it's exuberant shouts of victory with the clapping of hands and dancing, the Lord is pleased when we pour out whatever is in our "alabaster jar of ointment" in our love for him.

In **Luke 5:17-26** there was a certain church meeting being held in someone's home. The crowd was so thick in the house, and the power of the Lord Jesus Christ was so present, that anyone with a need knew they would have it met. It says in **verse 17** that the power of the Lord was present to heal people. However, in the crowd of the house were Pharisees and teachers of the law, who were blocking this power to heal like walls that prevent the waterfalls of justice and stop up the mighty streams of righteousness. These men had memorized the first five books of the Old Testament, and while these first five books taught them about the Lord Jesus Christ as the messiah who was to come, they did not recognize him as the One they had read about and their Healer. Instead, they were sitting and listening to him in order to trap him in his words. The very one that they had learned about was standing in their presence with his power there, ready to meet their needs. However, because they didn't even think that they had a need, they were going to miss out on healing!

Now, there was a man who was in this vicinity who was paralyzed. This man's friends came into his house, and said that they were going to carry him into the very presence of God. Now, there may have been people around him that doubted, but both the man and his friends were undeterred. They carried him from his home, and to the house meeting, because that's where the Lord was, and he is the waterfalls of justice and the mighty streams of righteousness! So, we see that one powerful question to ask as we approach Christ the Healer is, "Are we carrying each other into the presence of Jesus Christ?

Testimony- Love lifted me!

I remember when, at the age of 16, before I knew Jesus as my personal Savior, a certain boy named Pete in my school told me he was praying for me. We were in the same Advanced Biology class together, and before the school bell would ring to start class, he would often share the good news about the Lord from a little New Testament and tell me that he was praying for me. In fact, as I found out later, Pete had his entire youth group praying for me weeks before I received Jesus and surrendered to Him as Lord my Life.

I sometimes wonder what would have happened had this one boy with compassion for my soul and others who cared about my eternal future, not prayed for me. I do not know for sure what would have happened, but I am so very thankful that the Lord motivated them to pray for me, and that they listened. The Love of God has been poured forth into our hearts by the Holy Spirit, and Pete used it to bring me, his friend, to the Lord's eternal salvation!

Another one of the Holy Spirit's many ministries is to burden us to pray in intercession for the lost. Once I received Christ as my Savior in April of 1975, and then was baptized on May 25th, 1975, the Lord began to put several lost friends on what I call my prayer radar, just as he had put me on Pete's. Now, I have made it a part of my daily intercession time to lift up many acquaintances and family members who don't yet know Jesus personally. I have seen God's mercy and faithfulness in people's lives because of these times of carrying the burden of loved souls to the Great Shepherd.

Three groups regarding healing.

You see, there are always at least these three groups in any church setting regarding this issue of Divine Healing. They are; the crowd around the house, the Pharisees and teachers of the law, and the friends of the paralyzed man.

- **Religious Crowds:** The religious crowds are not out of line. In fact, they were in the right place at the right time to hear the Master, and by listening they were doing what they should have. But yet, it was the crowd that kept this man from meeting the Lord Jesus Christ and getting his healing. The man's friends at first tried to get the crippled man in the front door, but they couldn't because of the crowd. So what did they do? Did they stop seeking the source of Healing? Absolutely not! What did they do? They resolutely said that they were going to get into the presence of the Lord. They didn't care what it took, for they loved the one with a desperate need. The sick man, as you could imagine, was suggesting that perhaps they take him in through the window, but the friends had their eyes on higher entrances. They knew that there is a roof of access from above. "A roof?," thought the invalid. Is a roof not supposed to keep people and things out of a home? Yes, but when it comes to accessing the Healer, it is sometimes necessary to be considered radical in the eyes of others. Now, when I say they did something radical, I don't mean off the deep end and unscriptural. What radical means here is that they did something that nobody had ever done before. No one had ever gone up on a roof, taken the tiles apart, and dropped a needy friend down into hands of the Healer! They lowered the man. Just picture lowering a man into your church, in front of the preacher while he is busy teaching! Well, you would cause a big stir to say the least! The teachers and the Pharisees were listening and waiting to trap him. The crowd is also there listening, but only these friends had the faith to bring the man into the Lord's presence for healing to be applied.

- **Friends:** When the friend was dropped in front of the Lord, the Bible says Jesus "saw their faith." It also emphasizes the importance of faith by stating that without faith it's impossible to please God. We know that the Lord was pleased and delighted to see this breaking up of the roof, for it was truly representative of the unplowed ground of the hearts. How much more of an example can we give of breaking up unplowed ground than going up on a roof and lowering a man into the presence of the Lord? He looked at them, and when he saw their faith, he said "Son, your sins are forgiven you."

• **Pharisees:** Right away the Pharisees and the teachers of the law, the most religious figures of their day, thought that it was blasphemy. "How can this man forgive sins," they thought? Only God can do that! Well, little did they know, that, in fact, it was God who was talking. He went on to say that it's easier to say your sins are forgiven, than it is to say "be healed" and to have it happen. So that all would know Jesus has the power to forgive and save, he said for him to take up his mat and go; immediately, the man took up his mat and walked home!

The whole crowd was amazed! They gave praise to God. They said they'd never seen anything like this before. However, the Pharisees and the teachers of the law did not praise God. Their jealousy and anger blocked the waterfalls of justice and the mighty streams of righteousness from even trickling down on their souls.

God can not deny himself, nor can his healing nature be denied. This is such an empowering thought, when you apply it to the love that he has for you and I and how He really wants to heal you! Think of this- God not being able to deny himself includes that He can not deny his healing nature. It is going to be expressed. Why is this? Well, God's love for us is a part of his unchanging nature and healing his children an unchanging part of his will. Meditate on the reality that there is nothing you can do to earn more, and nothing you can do to diminish this healing love for you.

We were all like sheep that went astray. Every one of us has turned to our own selfish ways like the Pharisees did in the passage above. In being born into this world with a sinful nature, and in choosing to turn our backs on the Father, we become like the prodigal son. God's remedy? He who knew no sin, the Lord Jesus Christ, was made to be a sin offering for us, that we might be made the righteousness of God in Christ Jesus. He was wounded for our transgressions, he was bruised for our iniquities, the chastisement of our peace was upon Him, and with His stripes we are healed. God has laid on Jesus the sins of the world, and thereby was in Christ Jesus reconciling the world unto him. In Jesus, we now have redemption through his blood, which includes healing. Jesus is the Only Way to be saved.

In **John 14:6** we read, "Jesus saith unto him, 'I am the way, the truth, and the life: no man cometh unto the Father, but by me.'"

Again, in **1 Timothy 2:5-6** we see the same truth: "For *there is* one God, and one mediator between God and men, the man Christ Jesus; who gave himself a ransom for all, to be testified in due time."

This is the Heavenly Father sending his Son, Jesus, to pay the price for our souls. God valued you so much he gave His own blood to purchase you, both mind, body, soul, and spirit.

Will you take time right now to stop and thank God for loving you loyally? Thank Him for not letting you go on your own stubborn and selfish ways, but for stopping you from you life of sin to give you his eternal life through faith in Jesus Christ! Our Father in heaven actually loved you from before the foundation of the world. Yes, he knew you, chose you, and loved you before He even spoke the world into existence. Therefore, join me in thanking God for this unchanging love that caused him to include you in His eternal plan. This love caused him to send his one and only Son Jesus, in order to take your place on the cross; then it caused him to reveal himself to you, and give you the faith to receive His grace in the great miracle of salvation!

Now that you have been saved by God's grace through faith, it is time to be rooted and grounded only in the love that Jesus has for you. Nothing else is sufficient for rooting and grounding in today's turbulent times. Yet, some try to be rooted in and grounded in things other than the love of God for them. Why is this?

Many of us were hurt as infants, children, and young people. Some of us were rejected, abused, or even abandoned physically. This abuse took many forms. Some were verbally lashed at by a parent's sharp tongue. Others were actually physically beaten or sexually abused. Jesus knows your scars from the past, and all mankind needs healing from one hurt or another. Today, let us come to Jesus who knows about all of this. Let us come to the Great Healer of soul and body who still loves you!

Today, he wants you to invite him to go back into your childhood or recent adulthood with you. In prayer, ask our loving Father to help you uncover the layers of bitterness, anger, distrust, fear, and other destructive emotions. This is a part of His loyal love and healing for you!

Today, some of us may not yet have received Jesus Christ as our Lord and Savior. You may be saying, "No, I am too young." Well, I ask you "Are you younger than six?" That was the age of my younger daughter, Alicia, who prayed to receive Jesus as her personal Lord and Savior and was baptized. Then after turning just ten years of age, Alicia jumped on her very first plane ride- a thirteen hour, non-stop flight, to Beijing, China, with her parents. We then testified and witnessed to the Chinese people! Are you that young?

You may be excusing your responsibility to surrender your life to Jesus by saying, "Now don't be silly! I'm too old to be of any use to God." Are you really too old? Are you older than Moses, who at eighty, yes eighty, had just begun his ministry?

Some who are reading may justify not following Jesus the Healer by saying, "No I can not be of any use to God, because I am not educated enough to even read. Or maybe you read, but have difficulty learning the Good News from the Bible. My friend, most of the mighty men and women used by God throughout all history were not people of high education, whether Peter, James, Andrew, or even myself without a college degree! We are accepted as we are, and used by God to bring Him all of the glory!

Others contemplating commitment to Christ have said, "No, I am poor. I am unemployed and don't have the adequate finances to even feed my own family." Others are employed, but still are barely surviving from month to month. So they say "When God is good enough to turn things better for me financially, then I will be able to serve God." Well, when Peter left his fishing business to follow Jesus, did he have plenty of assurance for future finances? No, not in the natural way of looking at financial security, by employment in a job. However, God supplied all of Peter's needs while he was faithful in the ministry. Jesus even sent him to the ocean one day to pull out a fish to pay his taxes! My God will supply all of your needs according to His riches in glory, as you seek first His kingdom and His righteousness.

Today is your day for being saved, and then being healed. Please bow your head after reading this and pray with me now something like this prayer: "Father, I come to you knowing that in your love for me, you sent your son Jesus to save me. I believe that he died for my sins, and that His blood takes my sins as I believe and confess Him. I confess that I am a sinner. I have sinned against you and I admit that I have no other source to help me but your mercy to forgiven me of all of my sins. I am so undeserving of your payment of all my debts, but believe that Jesus paid the price for them fully on the cross for me. So, as an act of my will, I decide to give up all of the control of my life, and ask you to forgive me and take the Lordship and control of my life! I believe you now have come into my heart, and that I have eternal life. I ask for the power of the Holy Spirit to fill me with love for you, your word, and your will. Father God, I

will obey you by first confessing you before men in public baptism. It is in Jesus' precious name that I pray. Amen!"
Congratulations! You are now saved, being healed in your spirit, and on the road to total wholeness. Surrendering your life to the Healer prepares you to be healed and experience all that our loving Lord Jesus Christ has destined for you.

Chapter Two-
Don't Blame God!

—+—

God gives only good gifts

In this age of rapid medical advancements, biotechnology, cloning, and DNA research why are God's people who have these promises suffering like never before? Well, to begin with, lets look to God's Word and see that God does not give this sickness or tragedy to you and your family. We will see from scripture that God does not teach his children or increase their character by making them sick or sending them early death.

- **James 1:17** " Every good gift and every perfect gift is from above, and cometh down from the Father of lights, with whom is no variableness, neither shadow of turning." No "variableness" means that God does not even waver slightly.

- **Matthew 7:7-11** "If ye then being evil know how to give good gifts unto your children, how much more shall your Father which is heaven give good things to him that ask Him?"

To translate this into a modern scenario, lets say that parents in the medical profession were giving their children access to blood samples with deadly diseases. This would cause an outrage, and state officials would surely have their children taken away. Yet, some say that our Heavenly Father, the Father and Creator of the whole human race, would send us sickness?

Have you become bitter or angry with God over sickness or tragedy, either yours or that of a loved one? Well, my dear friend, please realize that God is on your side for healing and is the lover of your soul. Put aside your anger, frustration, and uncertainty, and reunite with God as both your best friend and your doctor. It is time to get angry at the devil whom we will see is the author of sickness instead of God and then to start resisting him!

God is good all the time

- **Psalms 145:8-9** "The Lord is gracious and full of compassion, slow to anger and of great mercy. The Lord is good to all and full of mercy and his tender mercies are over all his works."

God is good all the time- all the time God is good. God cannot be, or do evil. In fact, Jesus said he made the rain to fall on the just and the unjust, and he sends his sun on the evil and the good. God is so full of goodness, mercy, and compassion, that he doesn't have enough of his own children to bestow it on; so, he's good to the ungodly. In **Matthew 9:27-28**, we see that healing is a mercy. It says, "When Jesus departed thence, two blind men followed him, crying and saying, 'Thou, Son of David, have mercy on us!' And when he was come into the house, the blind men came to Him, and Jesus said unto them, 'Believe thee that I am able to do this?' They said unto him, 'Yes, Lord!' Then touched He

their eyes, saying, 'According to your faith, be it unto you.'"
God is good to those who by an act of faith take refuge in
him. He spoke this through his prophet Nahum and it is still
true for us today.

- **Nahum 1:7** "The Lord is good, a stronghold in the
  day of trouble; and He knows those who trust (take
  refuge) in Him."

- **Seeds:** God made seeds (the Word of God), and
stands back and waits for man to plant them. If we take the
seed that God created and then men packaged, but put them
up on a shelf, the seeds won't do anything. Even if we cry
and plead for them to grow, they will not until we take them
off the shelf, plant them in faith, and walk away thanking
God that we have received a crop.

- **Refrigerators:** God has given us a refrigerator
full of food to nourish us. But, if we don't believe that we are
welcome to take from the already provided for goods, we'll
sit there and starve. It doesn't matter if children plead, beg,
or cry, no father will keep opening the door for his teenager
when he's told the child repeatedly that all he has is theirs
for the taking. Even so, our Heavenly Father has done everything he can do about our healing; it is now the child of God
that must believe, trust, act, and partake.

- **Letters announcing an Inheritance:**
Say your father leaves his elder son, your older brother, his
millions, but your brother predeceases you. So, you receive
a letter saying that your brother loved you so much that he
made you the heir of the fortune if anything happened to him.
Thus, you are told by the bank teller that there are millions in
the bank that have your name on them. You cannot receive
the gift without opening the letter (reading the Word of God),

believing the letter (believing that God can heal), and acting on it to withdraw the money (proclaiming your healing in the Name of Jesus.)

So, God's gift of healing to us is there, and we just have to take it. This truth is like planting seeds, opening the refrigerator, and receiving inheritances.

God's goodness is unchanging

- **Malachi 3:6** "For I am the Lord, I change not."
  Jehovah-Shammah is still "The Lord ever present."
  Jehovah-Jireh is still "The Lord our Provider."
  Jehovah-Nissi is still "The Lord our Banner or Victory."
  Jehovah-Shalom is still "The Lord our Peace."
  Jehovah-Raah is still "The Lord our Shepherd."
  Jehovah- Tsidkenu is still "The Lord our Righteousness."
  Jehovah- Rapha is still "The Lord our Healer or Doctor."
  (See Exodus 15:26)

- **Hebrews 13:8** "Jesus Christ the same yesterday and today and for ever."

The word for "same" found here in **Hebrews 13:8** is the Greek "**ho autos,**" and means "the very same identical person in every respect." My friend, nothing about God's healing nature has ever changed from the days of Jesus of Nazereth's earthly ministry. You can come to his throne of grace and ask confidently for healing because God is still Jehovah- Rapha which means "The Lord our Healer or Doctor."**(See Exodus 15:26)**

- **Hebrews 11:6** says that "God is the rewarder of those who diligently seek Him."

One of the first questions the incurable must ask themselves is "will I devote myself to seeking God and knowing him in all these eternal manifestations including The Lord as my Doctor?"

There is no sickness in Heaven

- **In Matthew 6:9-11** Jesus taught us to pray a model prayer which included the words, "Thy kingdom come, thy will be done, on earth as it is in heaven." So, just what is the will of God in heaven at this very moment? Whatever it is concerning the healing of our bodies, that is what we are to be praying for.

- **Revelation 21:4** reveals a picture of the heavenly reality. "And God shall wipe away all tears from their eyes and there shall be no more death; neither sorrow, nor crying, neither shall there be any more pain, for the former things are passed away." You can pray that this will of God be a reality in your life and that God wipe away the death, sorrow, crying, and pain. They can be a "former thing" now in this life for you!

- **1 John 5:14-15** is the basis for your confidence in praying for healing today. "And this is the confidence (faith, or cheerful and joyful courage) that we have in him, that if we ask any thing according to his will he heareth us: and if we know that he hear us, whatsoever we ask, we know that we have the petitions that we desired of him."

Testimony- Mrs. Dodie Osteen's healing from cancer

When Mrs. Dodie Osteen (mother of Joel Osteen of Lakewood Church in Houston TX) was diagnosed with metastatic liver cancer in December of 1981, the Christian doctor gently told her husband, evangelist John Osteen, that she only had a few weeks to live, with or without chemotherapy. They ran every test known to man but could not find the primary tumor. This is surely an example of what we are hearing many call "incurable organ disease."

Mrs. Osteen says, in her book entitled "Healed from Cancer," that the hospital sent her home to die, but she had other plans. She prayed the prayer of faith, and, in agreement with her husband, they took authority together against the cancer and against all the cancer cells; John Osteen also anointed her with oil in the Name of Jesus. Then she rose up and went on with life to live as a healed woman! That was December 11, 1981.

"My first morning home I got up, bathed and put on a dress that now swallowed my 89 pound frame. I was not going to act sick," Dodie says in her book. This faith filled woman put a photo of herself in her wedding dress and of her riding a horse on vacation in front of her to visualize her happiest and healthiest days. She used **Isaiah 43:26,** which states, "Put me in remembrance; let us contend together; state your case, that you may be acquitted," to remind Jesus in the middle of the night, "Jesus, I don't want to die, I will not die, but live and declare the works of the Lord." **Psalms 118:17** Dodie reminded the Lord that her husband and children needed her and that He needed her also to do His will here on the earth. She examined her heart for sin, and the Lord dealt with her to write seven letters to people, including her husband, children, and friends, whom she felt she had offended in the early part of her illness because she had been so irritable. She also made it a point to pray for other people's healing, for she found that in giving of herself in her time of need, her healing came more quickly. **Luke 6:38,**"Give and it shall be given unto you," was the truth she based this upon.

She held fast her confession of healing according to **Hebrews 10:23,** "Let us hold fast the profession of our faith without wavering; for he is faithful that promised." Dodie read and confessed the Scriptures daily, even though she sometimes felt her faith was wavering. What she discovered from the Lord was that her wavering was in her head and not in her heart. The enemy tried to condemn her for wavering in her head, but she resisted the discouragement and kept her faith in her heart. By casting down imaginations that tried to bring fear, she laughed at symptoms, even though she is a RN and understood what wasn't functioning properly. She kept battling the disease with quotes from the Word of God on healing, and said that if she had had any doubt that it was God's will for her to be healed she never would have lived.

One day when they left for a service, Dodie's husband, John, left his Bible laying open on the bed. When they returned, he heard the pages of the Bible turn by what seemed to be a visitation by an angel. Looking over, he saw the page had changed to **Psalms 105:37,** and he read, "He brought them forth also with silver and gold: and there was not one feeble person among their tribes." What encouragement from the Lord!

Her children treated their mother as a healthy, normal mom, doing things such as expecting her to do the laundry and cook, etc. This kept her from throwing "pity parties," and so she would command her body to get going and do these tasks that all healthy mothers do.

Two years later in November, 1983 a blood test confirmed complete healing from metastatic liver cancer!

Jesus on earth - God's will in action as he healed all.

- **Matthew 4:23-24** "Teaching, preaching, healing all manner of sickness and all manner of disease among the people."

- **Matthew 8:16-17** "When the evening was come, they brought unto Him many that were possessed with devils, and he cast out the spirits with his word and healed all that were sick. That it might be fulfilled which was spoken by Isaiah the prophet saying, "Himself took our infirmities and bare out sicknesses."

- **Matthew 9:35-36** "All the cities and the villages teaching, preaching the gospel of the Kingdom and healing every sickness and every disease among the people. He was moved with compassion on them."

- **Matthew 12:15** "He withdrew himself from thence and great multitudes followed him and he healed them all."

- **Matthew 14:34-36** "Came into the land of Gennesaret. When the men of that place had knowledge of him they sent out into all that country round about and brought all that were diseased and besought him that they might only touch the hem of his garment and as many as touched were made perfectly whole.."

- **Matthew 15:30-**" And great multitudes came unto him, having with them those that were lame,

blind, dumb, maimed, and many others, and cast
them down at Jesus' feet and he healed them."

Jesus wants to heal all of your sicknesses and diseases
today and there is no sickness or disease too difficult for
Jesus to heal you of today!

- **Deut. 7:15** "The Lord will take away from you
  ALL sickness and will afflict you with none of the
  terrible diseases of Egypt which you have known
  but will lay them on all those who hate you."

Jesus rebuked sickness the same way He rebuked evil spirits.

- **Luke 4:31-39** "And Jesus came down to
  Capernaum, a city of Galilee, and taught them
  on the sabbath days. And they were astonished at
  his doctrine: for his word was with power. And
  in the synagogue there was a man, which had a
  spirit of an unclean devil, and cried out with a
  loud voice, saying, 'Let us alone; what have we
  to do with thee, thou Jesus of Nazareth? Art thou
  come to destroy us? I know thee who thou art;
  the Holy One of God.' And Jesus rebuked him,
  saying, 'Hold thy peace, and come out of him.'
  And when the devil had thrown him in the midst,
  he came out of him, and hurt him not. And they
  were all amazed and spake among themselves,
  saying, 'What a word is this: for with authority
  and power he commanded the unclean spirits,
  and they come out.' And the fame of him went
  out into every place of the country round about.
  And he arose out of the synagogue, and entered
  into Simon's house. Simon's wife's mother was

taken with a great fever; and they besought him for her. And he stood over her, and rebuked the fever, and it left; she immediately arose and ministered unto them.

Here we see that when Jesus came into the city of Galilee, he taught them on the Sabbath day, and they were astonished at His word, for it was with power and authority. In the synagogue, there was a believer who had a demon. At least we think it was a believer but at least it was a person in a location where believers met who had a spirit of a devil. It cried out in a loud voice, saying things like, "Let us alone; what have we to do with you, Jesus of Nazareth? Have you come to destroy us?" It said this last phrase, because the devil and his demon forces know that their eternal punishment is certain in the time to come, as we read in **Revelation 21:8**. This demonic spirit went on to say, "'And I know who you are- the Holy one of God.'" Jesus rebuked him; notice the word rebuke here. What Jesus did is "rebuke" and it is not a kind, gentle word, but harsh, forceful, powerful, and authoritative. That authority and the power to back it up that our Lord Jesus has is like the badge and gun of a policeman. It is like the authority given a State Trooper from the State Government, and is like having the power of an automatic weapon to back up that badge whenever needed! For us, it is the Name of Jesus that is our invisible spiritual badge, and we should wear it to use it. Our weapons are mighty through God to the pulling down of the devil's strongholds including that of sickness and disease. This power is of the Holy Spirit, which backs up the authority in the Name of Jesus.

Then, in this same Luke chapter 4 passage we see that Jesus went to the house of Simon Peter's mother, who had a great fever. Jesus stood over her, and rebuked the sickness out of her. The word in both passages for **"rebuked"** is the same, **"epitomize,"** which depicts an "I- hate-you" reaction. This harsh reaction is the way you would act toward a mangy, tick-infested dog trying to come in your house, or a thief breaking in to steal from you and harm your family. So are you beginning to see how Jesus felt about sickness and diseases on his people?

All God's promises are yes and Amen

- **2 Corinthians 1:20** says, "For all the promises of God in him (Christ) are yea, and in him (Christ) Amen, unto the glory of God by us."

When God gave sinful people like us the miracle of new birth, and our entire past was put under his cleansing blood, we were given a new heart of flesh for the old heart of stone. If he did all that for us when we were sinners, how much more would he do today as a Father who loves his children for healing of our "outer shell." You do not have to die of this ailment! You can trust these promises of God and claim them as God speaking directly to you today. God is not a man. He cannot lie or fail for according to His very nature this is impossible.

- **Psalms 118:17** "I shall not die, but live and declare the works of the Lord."

- **Numbers 23:19-20** "God is not a man that he should lie, neither the son of man that he should repent; hath he said it, and shall he not do it? Or hath he spoken, and shall he not make it good?" "Behold, I have received commandment to bless, and He hath blessed and I can not reverse it."

- **Joshua 21:45** "Not a word failed of any good thing which the Lord had spoken. All came to pass."

Satan - the author of sickness is evil and kills, steals and destroys.

Listen to how Jesus described Satan as your enemy who is a thief:

- **John 10:10** "The thief cometh not but for to steal, kill, and destroy. I am come that they might have life and have it more abundantly."

Jesus came to give us so much life that our cup overflows and those around us are also able to enjoy the overflow! Sickness is not life overflow. Sickness steals life. Satan is the source of sickness because he brought sin into the world. Remember, it was Satan that deceived Eve and thereby brought sin into the human nature and experience.

- **Romans 5:12** "Wherefore, as by one man sin entered into the world, and death by sin; and so death passed upon all men, for that all have sinned."

When you realize that sickness is a slow form of death and that death came from sin, you will hate and resist sickness like you should resist sin. This is like a "unholy trinity". It is time to resist sin, sickness, and their author Satan with equal fervor! Since sickness and physical death is the direct result of sin and because Satan is the direct author of sin, sickness, and death, we should treat them all the same. Resist them, rebuke them, and refuse to put up with them!

God says that the works of the devil are both sin and sickness.

In **1 John 3:8,** it says, "For this purpose the Son of God was manifested, that he might destroy the works of the devil."

Hebrews 2:14 also states that Jesus' death destroyed the works of the devil, saying, "Forasmuch then as the children are partakers of flesh and blood, he also himself likewise took part of the same; that through death he might destroy him that had the power of death, that is, the devil."

So then, because in **John 19:30**, Jesus said, "It is finished," we can know that Christ has destroyed the devil's works as it pertains to his believers, thus destroying Satan's power over death!

Jesus annulled the power of sickness and oppression.

- **Acts 10:38** "Now God anointed Jesus of Nazareth with the Holy Ghost and power; who went about doing good, and healing all that were oppressed of the devil; for God was with him."

Here we can see two things in that:

God anointed Jesus of Nazareth with the Holy Ghost and with power. Thus, we cannot say that the healings in the Bible were simply because Jesus was the second person in the Trinity. Jesus did not do one miracle until he was baptized in the power of the Spirit in the Jordan River. The great encouragement we gain from this reality is that we Christ's followers have the same Holy Spirit anointing us too!

1 John 2:20, "But ye have an unction (or anointing) from the Holy One, and ye know all things."

1 John 2:27, "But the anointing which ye have received of him abideth in you......"

Then, all those who Christ cured on earth had been oppressed of the devil. The word oppressed" here is "**kataku-**

nasteuomenous" which comes from two words: "**kata**" meaning "down" or "under" and "**dunasteuo**" meaning "to hold power or exercise lordship over". Those Christ cured according to God, writing through Luke the beloved physician here in **Acts 10:38,** were under domination, or being held down, by Satan.

Sickness is bondage not blessing

> **Luke 13: 10-16** says, "And he (Jesus) was teaching in one of the synagogues on the Sabbath. And, behold, there was a woman which had a spirit of infirmity for eighteen years, and was bowed together, and could in no wise lift up herself. And when Jesus saw her, he called her to him, and said unto her, 'Woman, thou art loosed from thine infirmity. And he laid his hands on her; and immediately she was made straight, and glorified God. And the ruler of the synagogue answered with indignation, because Jesus had healed on the Sabbath day; he said unto the people, 'There are six days in which men ought to work; in them, therefore come and be healed, and not on the Sabbath.' The Lord then answered him, and said, 'Thou hypocrite, doth not each one of you on the Sabbath loose his ox or his ass from the stall, and lead him away to watering? And ought not this woman, being a daughter of Abraham, whom Satan hath bound, lo these eighteen years, be loosed from this bond on the Sabbath day?'"

Concerning the phrase, "which had a spirit of infirmity" the word "**infirmity**" is the greek word, "**astheneia.**" It is the most common word in the Greek language for "sickness." For 18 years this woman, a daughter of Abraham, was being held in bondage by a "spirit of sickness." How could sickness be of God when Jesus said that satan had bound this woman with a spirit?

Disease spirits

Also, in **Mark 9:25** Jesus rebuked another foul spirit of sickness. Jesus treated this as a personal demon being sent to make the person both deaf and dumb. Many sicknesses and diseases need a good rebuking in Jesus' name to expel a demonic spirit behind them. My experience with asthma, for example, is that it is also a spirit to be resisted in faith in Jesus' name. According to **James 4:7** when you, "Submit yourselves therefore to God and resist the devil, he will flee from you."

Testimony- the spirit of asthma cast out brings healing

In Chicago, I was ministering in a small Indian church where they speak Malayalam which is the language of the southwest province of Kerela I have visited. A beautiful little girl, about 8 years old, came forward with her parents. The pastor told me she had been diagnosed with asthma. At that same time I felt the healing anointing of the Holy Spirit flow like electricity coming through my arm into my hand. The Lord said in my heart, "Cast it out." Therefore I spoke to the asthma spirit and commanded it to leave the little girl in the Name of Jesus. A few weeks later, I received a phone call from the pastor of that church stating that the parents had taken their daughter back to the doctor and that doctors could find no trace of asthma in her.

Satan smote Job

Often people point out Job as an example of those of God's children that He wants to suffer sickness for His glory or for some other mysterious and unknown reason. Who smote Job? Have you really looked closely at the full story of both Job's sickness and his healing?

> **Job 2:7** "So went Satan forth from the presence of the Lord and smote Job with sore boils from the sole of his foot unto his crown."

Who smote Job? Satan did it. Could he do it without God's permission? No. God gave Satan permission to smite Job with sore boils. In fact, God pointed out Job.

> **Job 42:10** "And the Lord turned the captivity of Job, when he prayed for his friends: also the LORD gave Job twice as much as he had before."

Wow! Job was both healed and prospered by God after satan had smitten him with sore boils from the sole of his foot unto his crown.

Testimony- God's help comes through doctors and prayer

When I was in India recently, I cracked a molar, and the cracked section of my tooth that remained was sharp and stuck in my tongue. At four in the morning after this happened, my tongue was very inflamed and my whole throat was becoming swollen from the resulting infection. I was supposed to teach twelve times throughout this province in the week ahead. The devil woke me up that morning, telling me, "You are going to die here in India, you old hypocrite. You are six thousand miles from your home and your family. You got here out of the will of God, and I'm going to get your cracked tooth so infected that you're going to die." I had to really wrestle in a spiritual warfare with the devil throwing his fear at me. I was saying, "Devil, I rebuke you. In the Name of Jesus, it is written, "I shall not die, but I shall live and declare the works of the Lord. " from **Psalms 118:17.** I continued, "With long life my Father will satisfy me. I resist you Satan, in the Name of Jesus." I was calling out fear and a spirit of infection, and commanding them to leave me.

By God's grace, I woke up that morning and drove two hours to a village to preach under the power of God. My throat opened up enough while I was teaching so that I could speak. Then, after I was done speaking, my throat closed back up, to the point that I could barely whisper. It was nine o'clock that evening, and I was supposed to preach ten more times that week. So, I said to my pastor, Moses Navgire, "Are there any good doctors in Daund on Sunday nights?" He told me he had one for me, and so we went right to the doctor's home. This Indian doctor pulled out a flashlight, the type you have in a toolbox, and looked down my throat. He spoke in Marahti as he looked, and then prescribed me four medications all written in Marahti and only costing $1.50 in the U.S. Now I really was releasing all kinds of faith concerning both the throat and tongue ailments and these unknown medications, for who knows what reactions I might experience from them? I trusted God to use both the natural medications and the supernatural power of His Spirit.

Praise the Lord that six hours later, my throat was open, and I was blessed with a fine Indian dentist who filed down the tooth's sharp edges. In addition to the help from my India doctor and pharmacist, I was able to speak ten more times! Many souls came to Christ and were healed that week. In my weakness, God's power was made strong. So, like I did at that time, you have a choice today. You can will to choose life, depend upon God's many avenues of healing and you will live! As Jesus asked the invalid in **John 5**, "Wilt thou be made whole?" In other words, the first issue is do you really want to be freed from this ailment? Also, we see from Jesus' question to the invalid at the Pool of Bethsaida that healing from Jesus is a clear choice we make. In **Deuteronomy 30:19**, "I call heaven and earth as witnesses today against you, that I have set before you life and death, blessing and cursing; therefore choose life, that both you and your descendants may live."

Scriptures on using the authority in the mighty Name of Jesus!

The following are some passages that you can meditate on each day to build your faith:

Ephesians 1:17 "That the God of our Lord Jesus Christ, the Father of glory, may give unto you the spirit of wisdom and revelation in the knowledge of him."

1:18 "The eyes of your understanding being enlightened; that ye may know what is the hope of his calling, and what the riches of the glory of his inheritance in the saints,

1:19 And what is the exceeding greatness of his power to us-ward who believe, according to the working of his mighty power,

1:20 Which he wrought in Christ, when he raised him from the dead and set him at his own right hand in the heavenly places,

1:21 Far above all principality, and power, and might, and dominion, and every name that is named, not only in this world, but also in that which is to come;

1:22 And hath put all things under his feet, and gave him to be the head over all things to the church,

1:23 Which is his body, the fullness of him that filleth all in all."

Ephesians 2:4 "But God, who is rich in mercy, for his great love wherewith he loved us."

2:5 "Even when we were dead in sins, hath quickened us together with Christ, (by grace ye are saved;)

2:6 And hath raise us up together, and made us sit together in heavenly places in Christ Jesus;

2:7 That in the ages to come he might shew the exceeding riches of his grace in his kindness toward us, through Christ Jesus."

You can clearly see from these passages in Ephesians that if you are a believer in Jesus you are seated with Christ and have authority in Him far above all principality, and power, and might, and dominion, and every name that is named, not only in this world, but also in that which is to come; This includes the fact that you as a Christ follower have authority over all sickness and disease, which is also far below your feet for you are in the body of Christ!

Philippians 2:5 "Let this mind be in you, which was also in Christ Jesus:

2:6 Who being in the form of God, thought it not robbery to be equal with God,

2:7 But made himself of no reputation, and took

upon him the form of a servant, and was made in the likeness of men;

2:8 And being found in fashion as a man, he humbled himself, and became obedient unto death, even the death of the cross,

2:9 Wherefore God also hath highly exalted him, and given him a name which is above every name,

2:10 That at the name of Jesus every knee should bow, of things in heaven and things in earth, and things under the earth;

2:11 And that every tongue should confess that Jesus Christ is Lord, to the glory of God the Father."

Acts 3:1 "Now Peter and John went up together into the temple at the hour of prayer, being the ninth hour."

3:2 "And a certain man lame from his mother's womb was carried, whom they laid daily at the gate of the temple which is called Beautiful, to ask alms of them that entered into the temple." (This man's lameness from birth was what we would call today an "incurable ailment" remember.)

3:3 "Who seeing Peter and John about to go into the temple asked an alms."

3:4 "And Peter, fastening his eyes upon him with John, said, Look on us."

3:5 "And he gave heed unto them, expecting to

receive something of them."

3:6 "Then Peter said, silver and gold, have I none; but such as I have give I thee; In the name of Jesus Christ of Nazareth rise up and walk."

3:7 "And he took him by the right hand, and lifted him up; and immediately his feet and ankle bones received strength."

3:8 "And he leaping up stood, and walked, and entered with them into the temple, walking, and leaping, and praising God."

3:9 "And all the people saw him walking and praising God;

3:10 And they knew that it was he which sat for alms at the Beautiful gate of the temple; and they were filled with wonder and amazement at that which had happened unto him."

Acts 3:16 "And His name, through faith in his name, hath made this man strong, whom ye see and know; yea, the faith which is in him hath given him this perfect soundness in the presence of you all."

According to Jesus in **Matthew 18:18,** let us who believe in Jesus Name pray the prayer of loosing the Holy Spirit's truth that builds faith for healing. Right now, let faith arise in your heart, and then pray the prayer of binding all interfering, hindering, and oppressing spirits.

Scriptures on using the power of Jesus' blood

Now cover yourself with the living Blood of Jesus based on these Bible truths:

Colossians 2:15 The Blood disarmed and made a spectacle of Satan at the cross. "And having spoiled (or disarmed) principalities and powers, he made a shew of them openly, triumphing over them in it (the cross.)

1 John 3:8 The Blood destroyed the works of the devil at the cross. "For this purpose the Son of God was manifested, that he might destroy the works of the devil."

Hebrews 2:14 "Forasmuch then as the children are partakers of flesh and blood, he also himself likewise took part of the same; that through death he might destroy him that had the power of death, that is the devil;

2: 15 And deliver them who through fear of death were all their lifetime subject to bondage."

So, you see that the Blood destroyed the works of the devil at the cross and our God is the solution to our physical needs. The Lord is our shepherd, you shall not lack. He makes you lie down in calm, peaceful, green pastures, and soothes your soul with calm, tranquil waters. His rod of authority, and his staff of power comfort you. Though you walk through, not stopping or being kept in, the valley of the shadow of death, you will fear no evil says God through the Shepherd, David in **Psalms 23.** As Job said, "That which I feared greatly came upon me." Fear is a door opener; faith is a door closer.

For some of us, this is the first time we have read about such a clear distinction between our good God giving good gifts, and the evil enemy bringing sickness. For others of us we had heard that but need an encouraging reminder as we battle through the physical trial of our faith. In either case we know that God's Word is now going forth powerfully, as seed that in sincere seeking hearts will bear fruit. We know that this healing seed will bear healing fruit in your open heart! You can expect what Jesus said about the parable of the sower to become real in your life.

Therefore, let us now examine our hearts to make sure it is good soil for the seed of the Word of God. If you have harbored anger, frustration or unbelief toward the Father in heaven, now is the time to bow your head and pray something like this: "Father, I have been wrong because I did not know it was the devil that made me or others sick. I have been blaming you, and I am very sorry for it. I admit that I have been angry toward you about my current situation or about the loss of a loved one. I now release this bitterness to you, my loving Father in heaven. Forgive me. In Jesus name, Amen." Congratulations, my friend, for you have taken a powerful step toward your healing!

Chapter Three-
Healing is Yours Today from
Christ's Atonement

---+---

What God's written word the Bible says about our physical healing and health needs to become richly abiding in our hearts. It needs to impregnate our spirit with an understanding of the finished work of Christ, because the power of the Son of Righteousness comes from within us as believers. This is because we have the Healer, the Lord Jesus by his Holy Spirit dwelling in our hearts. That is where the healing begins. We are healed first within our spirit- our mind, soul, spirit, will, and emotions; then our body gets physical healing, for it is the outer shell.

In this Chapter we are going to go take a close look at the healing brought us 2000 years ago by the precious wounds of our Lord Jesus in his sufferings. It will be your responsibility to take that written report, and get a Spirit taught revelation in your heart which will then turn into the reality of bodily healing. Come with me into the book of Isaiah the prophet speaking about 700 years before Christ of his sufferings and his subsequent exaltation at the right hand of God.

- **Isaiah 52:13-14** "See, my servant will prosper; He will be highly exalted. Many were amazed when they saw Him, beaten and bloody, and so disfigured one could scarcely know he was a person."

These verses are prophetic words Isaiah received years before the coming of Christ. As he is lifted up in the Spirit, Isaiah is receiving many levels of prophetic insight much like one would see many mountain ranges from an airplane. Verse thirteen describes the resurrected, exalted Christ, while the very next verse brings it back to the cross.

The Truth about Christ's Sacrifice for our Healing

Jesus did not just suffer on the cross. Prior to his hanging on the cross for our sins, He offered his whole being to be beaten and whipped and scourged, spat upon, cursed at, his head to be pierced with the crown of thorns, and his beard to be pulled out . Why did he allow this torture, when really, he could have just gone to the cross and died for our sins. He went there so that by His wounds, which we see in **Isaiah 53: 13-14** were all over His body, you are healed! Every part of Christ was touched so that every part of our person can be healed.

By His complete sufferings we are entirely healed!

- **Matthew 27:26** "Pilate, when he had scourged Jesus, he delivered him to be crucified." The Roman soldiers used whips of leather and attached metal and bone to create horrible instruments that tore Christ's flesh and produced excruciating agony in our Lord Jesus.

- **Isaiah 50:6** "I gave my back to the smiters, and my cheeks to them that plucked off the hair: I hid not my face from shame and spitting." The cruel Romans also plucked out Jesus' whiskers by the roots and spat upon our Lord as prophesied in this Isaiah passage: Why? Let us find out.

He was despised and forsaken of men on the cross

- **Isaiah 53:2** "For he (Christ) shall grow up before Him (the Father) as a tender plant and as a root out of dry ground. He hath no form or comeliness, and when we shall see him there is no beauty that we should desire him."

On the cross, man saw no majesty, splendor, attractiveness or distinctive appearance that would make us desire Christ; there was no beauty on the cross.

- **Isaiah 53:3** "He is despised and rejected of men, a man of **sorrows (makob)** and acquainted with **grief (choli)**; and we hid as it were our faces from him. He was despised and we esteemed him not.

- **Isaiah 53:4** "Surely he (Christ) hath **borne (nasa)** our **griefs (choli)** and **carried** our **sorrows (makob.)**

<u>Makob</u>: When we look up the original Hebrew translation for the KJV word sorrow (makob) in Strong's Concise Concordance of the Bible, we see that it also translates to shades of meaning like anguish, affliction, grief, and pain. **Makob** as used in this passage means **literal bodily pain,**

as also seen in **Job 33:19**: "He is chastened also with **pain**" (See also **Jeremiah 51:8.**)

Now, unfortunately, in 1611, when the King commissioned the translators, they translated this passage with a reflection of their own personal beliefs against divine healing and therefore only translated this word as "sorrows".

<u>Nasa:</u> **Isaiah 53:4** shows this further. The word for borne, **Nasa, means to bear** in the sense of suffering punishment for something. It is used the same way in this verse for sickness as it is in **Isaiah 53:12**, just a few verses later, for sin.

- **Isaiah 53:12** "He (Christ) was numbered with the transgressors; and he **bore (nasa)** the sin of many."

In these two passages above, the emphasis is on the taking of something and bearing it to a far away place. We plainly see that Christ bore both our sins and sicknesses vicariously for you and I on the cross.

<u>Choli:</u> The word **choli** is from **chalah,** meaning **to be weak, sick, or afflicted in the body.** Time and time again throughout the Bible, this same word is translated bodily sickness and diseases of the body, not of the spirit. Unfortunately, most versions of the Bible have it translated into a grief of the spirit. The original word can be translated grief as well as malady, anxiety, calamity, disease, and sickness. This Isaiah passage should have been translated sickness but as mentioned before, in 1611, when the King commissioned the translators, they translated this passage with a reflection of their own personal beliefs against divine healing and therefore only translated this word as **"griefs"**. The following passages also show usages of **choli** translated as **bodily sickness:**

- **Deuteronomy 7:15** "The Lord will take away from thee all **sickness**.

- **Deuteronomy 28:61** "**every sickness and every disease**."

(See also **1 Kings 17:17, 2 Kings 1:2, 2 Kings 8:8**)

Sabal: **Sabal means carried;** so Christ carried our pains. It also means to bear something as a penalty or chastisement. You can see sabal being used in **Lamentations 5:7** and **Isaiah 53: 11,** "He shall see of the travail of his soul, and shall be satisfied. ...for he shall **bear their iniquities**." The emphasis is on the weight of the load borne.

Concerning the Healing ministry of Christ, the Holy Spirit makes it abundantly clear what he said here in Isaiah when in Matthew the apostle quotes the **Isaiah 53** passage.

- **Mathew 8:16-17** "When the evening was come, they brought unto him many that were possessed with devils: and he cast out the spirits with his word, and healed all that were sick: **That it might be fulfilled which was spoken by Isaiah the prophet, saying. "Himself took our infirmities, and bore our sicknesses**."

God makes it so very clear that Christ bore and carried our bodily ailments not just our spiritual sicknesses.

Some argue that this **Mathew 8:16-17** account states that Christ fulfilled Isaiah's prophecy before the cross in his earthly ministry on that specific day of healing. If this is the case then it was only for those at that time and not for all believers today. However, if we take this train of thought, there are some ridiculous outcomes of this kind of reasoning when applied to other passages in the Bible . For example we can see this is not what God meant in another such example of "fulfilled prophecy" found in Luke.

- **Luke 4:17-21**, "And there was delivered unto him the book of the prophet Isaiah. And when he had opened the book, he found the place where it was written, The Spirit of the Lord is upon me, because he hath anointed me to preach the gospel to the poor; he hath sent me to heal the brokenhearted, to preach deliverance to the captives, and recovering of sight to the blind, to set at liberty them that are bruised, To preach the acceptable year of the Lord. And he closed the book, and he gave it again to the minister, and sat down. And the eyes of all them there were in the synagogue was fastened on him. And he began to say unto them, This day is this scripture fulfilled in your ears."

Here is a wonderful prediction, which Christ fulfilled all through his ministry, not just there in Nazareth on that day. He still fulfills it throughout the entire church age by virtue of we his body. This was not just limited to that day he spoke those words in Nazareth and neither was the **Mathew 8:16-17** prophecy just a one time fulfillment before the cross.

Your healing - a past tense provision for current possession.

- **I Peter 2:24** "Who his own self bore our sins in his own body on the tree, that we, being dead to sins, might live unto righteousness, by whose stripes (**molopi**) ye were healed."

The word in **1 Peter 2:24**, "**stripes,**" is the word **molopi** and it is a singular noun. "Stripes" actually means "**bruise,**" because our dear Savior's back had been so terribly scourged that no one blow could possibly be distinguished from the other. Every spot on His back was so bruised and lacerated that it was just like one great bruise.

Had there been even one quarter inch of space between any two of the bruises, the Greek word here would have then read in the plural rendering it '**molopsi**' or "**bruises,**" not '**molopi**' which is singular for "**bruise.**" You see, the Jews had a law that no person should be given more than 40 stripes when flogged. The Romans, who carried out Jesus' punishment, had no such law, so they often scourged their victim until they bled to death. All this was for your healing today from even "incurable illness." Hallelujah!

- **I Peter 2:24** "Who his own self bore our sins in his own body on the tree, that, we, being dead to sin, should live unto righteousness, by whose stripes you were healed."

"**Healed,**" as used in this passage, is from the Greek word, "**iaomai**" and it always speaks of **physical healing** in each of it's twenty eight usage's in the New Testament. It is not just "spiritual healing" Christ has purchased for you, both spiritual and physical healing on the cross. Don't let people twist all these passages on physical healing into just "spiritual healing." Do not be robbed of the full gospel that is the full good news about a full redemption purchased for you on the cross of Christ!

All sicknesses and diseases - curses we've been redeemed from.

- **Galatians 3:13** "Christ hath redeemed us from the curse of the law, being made a curse for us."

In **Deuteronomy 28:15-68**, God tells of the curse that will be on anyone who disobeys His law. Well, we are all guilty of the breaking of the Law of God.

We all deserve to come under the curse of this broken Law. However, the passage above from Galatians is saying that Christ became this curse in our place, for every man who hangs on a tree is cursed. The word redeemed here is **exagorazo**, which means **"to purchase or redeem out from, or away from."** Just what is in this "curse of the law?" The Word of God tells us in great detail from the **Deuteronomy 28** passage:

- **Deuteronomy 28:15** "all these 'curses' (**katarai**) shall come on thee;" God then lists pestilence, consumption, fever, inflammation, botch of Egypt, emerods, scab, blindness, astonishment of heart: ......and every sickness and every disease which is not written in the book of this law."

Deuteronomy 28:15-68, together with **Galatians 3:13**, is your ticket into divine healing and health! This redemption from "every sickness and every disease" includes the one you are struggling with. Confess today with holy boldness the following truth, "This sickness is a curse of the Law and Christ has redeemed me from this sickness. It is not mine for I am redeemed from this sickness by my Christ having suffered it for me on the cross. In Jesus Name, Amen!"

The Blood of Jesus, the Lamb of God, brings physical benefits.

- **1 Corinthians 5:7** "...Christ our Passover is sacrificed for us."

Picture this: Christ, the Lamb of God, slain on the cross; in the mind of God, before the foundation of the world. Christ, there on the cross, was our own personal Passover Lamb. We read of the original Passover lamb in the following passage:

- **Exodus 12:7, 12-13** "And they shall take of the blood, and strike it on the two side posts and on the upper door posts of the houses...and when I see the blood, I will pass over you and the plague shall not be upon you to destroy you, when I smite the land of Egypt."

The Israelites actually sprinkled the blood of their spotless lamb on their door posts to save them from the wrath of God. Then the flesh of that Passover lamb was also to be eaten for its physical benefits.

Yes, 2000 years ago Christ's blood was shed to save us from the wrath of God, and then Christ's flesh was broken for our physical benefits!

The question is today will you by faith sprinkle the Blood of Jesus against the plague and then partake of all the physical benefits of faith in the Lamb of God?

The Spirit makes life in our bodies

- **Romans 8:11** "But if the Spirit of him that raised up Jesus from the dead dwell in you, he that raised up Christ from the dead shall also quicken (the Greek for this KJV word quicken is "**zoo-**

poiesei"; from "**zoe**" meaning **life** and "**poieo**" meaning **I make**) your mortal bodies by his Spirit that dwelleth in you."

According to the usage of "**zoopoiesei**" in other New Testament passages, this is not a reference to our **bodies** being given life in the future resurrection. When the body in resurrection is described then the Greek word "**nekros**," is used. "**Nekros**" is the word that signifies "**from the dead,**" when used. In the **Romans 8:11** passage, however, "**thnetos**" is used for **body**. When "**thnetos**" is used, it is never in reference to a dead body.

John Calvin's commentary on **Romans 8:11** confirms this rendering as follows: "The quickening of the mortal body here cannot refer to the resurrection of the saints, but must mean a giving of life to their bodies, while here upon earth, through the Spirit."

Here's a powerful application for our health today. We have the very same Holy Spirit dwelling in us- who raised Christ from the dead, who did all of Christ's miracles, Paul's miracles, and Peter's miracles! It is the work of the Holy Spirit to keep making life in these mortal bodies of ours, now, even while on the earth. Believe it and receive it!

Which report will you believe- the truth or what others say

When we boil down what we are learning from **Isaiah chapter 53** the basic question is this: what report will you believe? Do you believe God's report, or the report of the seminary professor, the contradicting report of the doctor, or perhaps your own parents or friends who say you shouldn't expect God to heal you of this ailment?

- **Isaiah 53: 1** "Who hath believed our report, and to whom is the arm of the Lord revealed?"

The word **"believed"** literally means **"amened."** Another way to ask this is, "Who has said amen to the hearing of the Word." Have you ever wondered what you really mean when you hear the Word, and then you say, "Yes!" or "Amen!"? That is the Holy Spirit within you saying, "Yes! That's my Word!" The Spirit of God within us witnesses to our spirit that that is truth that we are hearing. Thus the Word **"amen"** means **"so be it"**, or to **"be confirmed"**. You are saying that you will receive and hang onto what you are hearing because it's reliable and faithful. When you say amen, it also means, "I'm totally committed to that! I'm basing my life on this!

This truth from **Isaiah 53** must move from just the written **report** from the Word you are reading, and into a **revelation** to your spirit by the Holy Spirit, becoming a **reality** of healing in your body. A great example of this is the healing of Evelyn Schumacher, the editor of this book.

Testimony- Evelyn Schumacher

In the spring of 2006, after a routine colonoscopy, my doctor told me that I would have to have surgery to remove a large polyp. I learned that he would remove several feet of my intestine and the right side of the colon would be recreated. The medical name for this is a "right hemicolectomy." The surgeon further explained that even though early tests did not show any cancer, it could not be ruled out until the surgery was completed and tests were done. I was surprised when I heard this news, but I knew that my Heavenly Father, God, was not surprised and already had the plan made and executed on my behalf. I just had to go through the steps that were required. Well meaning people told me that since I was 65 years old healing would be long and difficult. My Father,

God, spoke into my spirit assuring me that he had it under control and I should listen only to him.

At the time I received this news, I was attending a seminar on healing taught by the author of this book. My boss, Dr. Mark Wood was hosting the seminar at his office. I learned the precepts taught. So, I began listening often to healing tapes, read the word, and prayed as many were praying for me. My finances were a cause for concern as well, because income from my job was essential for my support.

God was intricately involved from the beginning. The morning of my appointment with the surgeon, Dr. Wood and I were praying and talking. As we talked about when I would have surgery, the Lord put in my Spirit the specific date of the surgery. I told this to Dr. Wood before I left for my appointment with the surgeon. After talking to me, the surgeon told me the scheduling nurse would be in to ask when I wanted to have the surgery.

We had a date in mind, which took my son's schedule into account. But, the nurse did not come in to ask my opinion. She entered the room and told me the date of surgery. It was exactly the same as what God had put in my spirit. I was to learn after my release from the hospital that the staff and patients there had developed a virus. I was released just before this occurred and realized how God had protected me.

The day of my surgery went well. My pastor and several family members were at the hospital. Afterward, I went into a very deep sleep, and each time I awoke, the nurses would comment on how deeply I was sleeping. During this deep sleep, in my spirit, I could see healing activity going on in the colon area. I knew that a supernatural healing was taking place.

On the third day, the surgeon came in to my hospital room and said that I was several days ahead in my healing, and instead of going home in five-seven days after surgery,

I could go home on the fourth day. I went back to work part time two weeks after surgery and full time three and a half weeks after surgery. The projected time for me to be off work was six to eight weeks. The surgeon released me two weeks after surgery and said if all his patients were like me, he would be out of business.

In my opinion, God healed me supernaturally and also by the use of traditional medicine. I believe that getting the "Word of God" into my mind, spirit and body is what made the difference in the speed and the ease of my recovery. I would not let anyone speak negative words over my surgery and healing. I believed God's promises and spoke them often. My thoughts were always full of God's Word, not what man would say. This is when I realized that knowing God's word and how it relates to me is very important.

If I had not had these assurances from God, my faith would have been affected by the words of others.

In the area of my finances, God spoke into my spirit that I was to send $20.00 each to two different ministries. When I questioned him about saving that money for the time I would be off work, He reminded me that He was my provider. I did what I was instructed to do. God then provided through two different people the exact amount of the pay that I would have lost from not being able to work. Every bill was paid, and each need I had was met. God really is good all the time.

Based upon **John 14: 26-27** and **John 16:12-13**, you can pray right now for your God to give you this inner confidence that Evelyn Schumacher has from her knowledge of His healing Word.

- **John 14: 26-27** "But the Comforter, which is the Holy Ghost, whom the Father will send in my name, he shall teach you all things, and bring all things to your remembrance, whatsoever I have said unto you. Peace I leave with you, my peace I give unto you; not as the world giveth, give I unto you. Let not your heart be troubled, neither let it be afraid."

- **John 16: 12-13** "I have yet many things to say unto you, but ye can not bear them now. How be it, when he, the Spirit of truth, is come, he will guide you into all truth: for he shall not speak of himself; but whatsoever he shall hear, that shall he speak: and he will show you things to come."

Right now pray something like this, "Father, I thank you that by Jesus' wounds I am healed. He took my infirmities and bore my sicknesses, and I give them to Him right now in the name of Jesus! I believe that you hear me, because my healing is your desire. I receive my healing, and see myself healed from this day forward. Thank you Father, for I am healed right now by Jesus' precious wounds. In Jesus' name, amen!

Chapter Four-
Jesus Says "Healing is Easier!"

———+———

Jesus says that physical healing is easier than being born again and forgiven of all our sins! It is easier than we think, easier than we make it, and easier than everything else in the spirit realm that He has blessed us with. Healing is easy to God!

- **Mark 2: 9-11** "He preached the Word unto them. They came unto him bringing one sick of the palsy, which was borne of four. And when they could not come nigh unto Him for the press, they uncovered the roof where he was; and when they had broken it up, they let down the bed wherein the sick of the palsy lay. When Jesus saw their faith (both the sick man and the four friends), he said unto the sick of the palsy, 'Son, thy sins be forgiven thee.' But, there were certain of the Scribes sitting there and reasoning in their hearts, 'Why does this man speak blasphemies? Who can forgive sins but God only?' And immediately when Jesus perceived in His spirit that they so reasoned within themselves, he said unto them, 'Why reason you these things in your hearts?

Whether it is easier to say to the sick of the palsy, "Thy sins be forgiven thee;" or to say, "Arise, and take up thy bed, and walk?" But, that ye may know that the Son of man hath power on earth to forgive sins, (he saith to the sick of the palsy,) I say unto thee, "Arise, and take up thy bed, and to thy way into thine house.'" And immediately, he arose, took up the bed, and went forth before them all, in so much that they were all amazed and glorified God, saying, 'We never saw it all in this fashion.'"

The recreated, born again spirit you received when you were saved is like a total engine replacement; you see, you've been born again, recreated into the image of Christ. God saved you. He took the old engine out, that stony heart, and put in a new heart of faith and receptivity to the power of the gasoline of God. That was the greatest and "hardest miracle" in your life. If God did that for us, then how much easier is it to fix your body from dents, smudges, tar-stains, and all other ailments; it is much easier and less expensive to get a little paint job done than it is to get the whole engine replaced. If you've already gotten your heart recreated, then everything else, when measured in human terms, is "easier." To God, nothing is difficult.

Besides this statement of Jesus in **Mark 2:9-11**, in passage after passage in the Bible, God unites the forgiveness of our sins with the healing of our diseases. God does not separate his love into compartments, and he does not distinguish between His care for our mind, soul, spirit, relationships or finances, and His care for our bodies.

- **Psalms 103:3** "...who forgiveth all thine iniquities; who healeth all thy diseases."

- **3 John 2** "I pray, above all things, that you prosper and be in health, just like your soul prospers."

Your body and your finances will mirror what's in your mind, emotions, and will. Well then, why are more believers not walking in this healing today? That is the same question the disciples in Jesus' day asked when they could not heal a boy.

Laws of Healing – like genetics, electricity, and gravity

God is often viewed as an arbitrary dispenser of blessing who sits on a throne and decides whether to stamp yes or no on our prayer requests. Whether or not we admit it, we often fall into this snare of thinking that God is deciding what to do when we pray. But, this is untrue; God works by laws that He has established in the universe. For example, God has set certain laws in the natural realm that will be universally and consistently functioning, such as the law of genetics. The law of genetics, discovered by Gregor Mendel, included the understanding of nucleic acids; he found that these chemicals produce proteins within a cell. Mendel discovered this in 1860, but his discoveries were buried and went unpublished for forty years. Now, were the people of his time considered ignorant, or were they just not blessed with knowledge yet? In 1900, Mendel's laws of genetics were rediscovered, but it wasn't until 1953 that James Watson and Francis Crick discovered the most famous nucleic acid– DNA and its double helix. Now, did Watson and Crick's discovery make Mendel ignorant, or just not blessed with all the information about the laws of genetics? The answer is obvious- Mendel, a very intelligent man, had just not discovered all the information.

There is another very simple question we can ask concerning DNA. When we didn't know about DNA, was it still the blueprint of the human genetic code? Of course! This principle is also true for other natural laws of the universe; even if a person is not aware of them, they will operate. The law of gravity is always true, even if you are a born-again, spirit-filled Christian, and you step out of a tenth story window. Does God say, "Oh, there's one of my most precious saints. Michael, shut the switch off on gravity. He's accidentally stepped off his porch, and he's falling." Why doesn't God switch off gravity? He doesn't because six billion people would fly off the earth! So, a lot of times, when people have prayed for healing, but not understood the law of healing, they are finding themselves wondering, "Why am I falling?" It is because they didn't understand that the law of healing. Like the law of gravity, it is going to work every time, and God is not going to unplug the laws.Another example is the law of electricity. Electricity has been on the earth since God created; cavemen could have lit their caves. There is an electromagnetic field in the earth, and Benjamin Franklin, with his kite, happened to figure it out. This law always stands true; if you unscrew a light bulb and stick your finger in the socket, you would be electrocuted even if you prayed. Why? God established the law for the good of all mankind; he will not override it.

All we have to do is learn that Christ in you is the hope of your glory; Christ within you is the electricity already in the wall, meaning that it's always there even if you don't know about it. We don't need the anointed evangelist to come and pray for us. He can, and God would use him. He could have electricity bolts flying out of his hand, but if you don't receive it, and decide to light your life with it, you're never going to get the power. Electricity, like Christ in you, is the power that has already been generated by the power plant, and delivered (by his wounds you were healed); but, you could be healed in the realm of the Holy Spirit, with electricity flowing all around you, and you'd never learn to take an active faith and a point of contact and reach out as an act of your will and say, "When I touch that switch, I will receive power into my life. Father, heal me!"

Laws of Healing and The Law of Sowing and Reaping

- **Galatians 6:7-9** "Do not be deceived; God is not mocked. For whatever a man sows, this he will also reap. For the one who sows to his own flesh, shall from the flesh reap corruption. But he who sows to the Spirit, shall from the Spirit reap eternal life. And let us not lose heart in doing good, for in due time we shall reap if we do not grow weary."

The law of sowing and reaping works everywhere in the world, for every single seed, every day, period. The power of this law is that you can have absolute confidence; if you put corn seed in the ground, three things will happen: one, corn will pop up. Secondly, the corn will pop up after it was planted; and lastly, the crop will be bigger than the seed. God made seeds (the Word of God), and stands back and waits for man to plant them.

If we take the seed that God created and placed in a finished pack, but put them up on a shelf, the seeds won't do anything. Even if we cry and plead for them to grow, they will not until we take them off the shelf, plant them in faith (read the Word of God and keep it in our hearts), and walk away thanking God that we have received a crop. We have to make God's past tense provision our current day possession.

The Word of God, Jesus said, is the seed God uses to grow things in our lives. God grows healing in your body by planting healing seed in your inner man.

- **Psalms 107:20** "He sent his word and healed them."

- **Proverbs 4:20-22** "God's Word is health (medicine) to all your flesh." (If planted by meditation within your heart and watered by prayer!)

So, if you plant seed- Word on healing- in your heart, healing will pop up in your life; it will be more healing than you put in, and sprout up after you put it in. Remember, we see in **Isaiah 55:10-11** that the Word from your lips will not return empty to God, but will accomplish the purpose for which he sent it.

After the Word is planted in your heart, weed out unbelief!

- **2 Corinthians 10:3-5** "Though we live in the world, we do not wage war as the world does. The weapons we fight with are not the weapons of the world. On the contrary, they have the divine power to demolish strongholds. We demolish arguments, and every pretension that sets itself up against the knowledge of God. And we take captive every thought to make it obedient to Christ."

Now, so often we pop "by His wounds you were healed" into our hearts, feel pain, and then say, "Oh, there's no "corn seed" in me." You become a farmer who goes to his field, and digs the corn seed all up, saying, "There must not be any corn anymore." Storms are good for corn, unless you become afraid and let unbelief creep in. Farmers don't get scared when there's a storm around their crop; they plant it, and go away.

In failure, Jesus told disciples they had unbelief.

- **Matthew 17:19-21** "Then came the disciples to Jesus apart, and said, 'Why could not we cast him out?' And Jesus said unto them, 'Because of your unbelief: for verily I say unto you, If ye have faith as a grain of a mustard seed, ye shall say unto this mountain, "Remove hence to yonder place;" and it shall remove; and nothing shall be impossible unto you. Howbeit this kind goeth not out but by prayer and fasting.'"

Another thing we see in this passage is that you don't need a super abundant amount of faith; all you need is pure, childlike faith.

See in **Mark 9:24** where the father of the child said, "Lord, I believe; help thou mine unbelief." This should also be our prayer! Jesus did cast out the demon and heal the boy, even when his followers failed. Today it is still God's will to heal you, even if some fail to receive.

- **Romans 12:1-2** I beseech you therefore, brethren, by the mercies of God, that ye present your bodies a living sacrifice, holy, acceptable unto God, which is your reasonable service. And be not conformed to this world: but be ye transformed by the renewing of your mind that ye may prove what is that good, and acceptable, and perfect will of God."

You must look into your heart and weed out everything that opposes the truth. You must do this as an act of your own will, for God is not going to "weed" for us. Some may ask, "Why did Aunt

Susie die, after all she prayed." I don't know, but God is faithful to the law of sowing and reaping; if the weeds grow taller than the seeds, they can choke out the good crop. She may have been in pure faith, but allowed the doubts of symptoms, circumstances, theology, modern doubt, and community unbelief to crowd out the seed and choke it.

The Law of the Spirit of Life in Christ Jesus

- **Romans 8:2** "For the law of the Spirit of life in Christ Jesus hath made me free from the law of sin and death."

The law of sin and death is like the law of gravity. If we "step out into sin," it is similar to stepping out of a window-we will fall. The law of the Spirit of Life in Christ Jesus is like the powerful law of thrust and the law of lift on the wings of an aircraft. When you fly in a huge 747 airplane, you might be wondering or thinking, "How many tons is this thing? How long is the runway? Is it really going to get up?" Yes, it does lift off; but, does it deny the law of gravity? No, it doesn't deny it, just like we don't deny the reality of sickness or sin. The law of thrust and lift simply overrides the law of gravity because of its power, just like Christ has taken power over sickness by His wounds. The law of thrust to us is the joy of the Lord; it propels us into a life of strength. We see this in **Nehemiah 8:10**. Nehemiah said, 'Go, and enjoy choice food and sweet drinks, and send some to those who have nothing prepared. This day is sacred to our Lord. Do not grieve, for the joy of the Lord is your strength.'"

I used to think that the joy of the Lord was like a vitamin-you take it, and then the joy is inside of you. But, joy in you from Jesus will lift you above your current circumstances. We see this lifting power in **Zephaniah 3:17**. "The Lord thy

God in the midst of thee is mighty; he will save, he will rejoice over thee with joy; he will rest in his love, he will joy over thee with singing."

This is the song of the bridegroom, Jesus. He is happy when he looks at you, and he sings. Yes, Jesus is very happy about you, and it is his joy that you take as a healthy remedy.

It is the generator of your healing. It is not joy brought on by your singing that heals you, but his singing in you that strengthens you and thereby heals. It is Christ in you that is the hope of glory. When you realize how much he loves you, it will be easier for you to understand the process of your healing. The Proverbs say, a merry heart does good like a medicine in **Proverbs 17:22** In another place it states that a merry heart makes a cheerful countenance. They also say that pleasant words are healing to your bones. In this truth, we find that the mind and the tongue are avenues for healing. God created the mind and the tongue for you to think and speak healing to your body. Psychosomatic and placebo effects are well known in medical science. For example, even if your doctor performs a totally useless therapy or treatment, but does it with high expectations and conveys those expectations of good results to you, studies show that you will cure quicker. That fact shows the power of positive expectations or natural faith.

Testimony- Greg Pettys

When I was eleven years old, living in Bangkok, Thailand, the Devil tried to snuff my life out with spinal meningitis. I had a temperature of 102-104 degrees Fahrenheit for three days; they had to put me in a tub full of ice cubes. I was going to die. They sent me to a hospital in Bangkok, and I'll never forget the nurses doing two spinal taps in one day with local anesthesia. These nurses had me on my side, sticking my spine with a hypodermic needle to withdraw fluid that was about to burst my skull because of the level of inflammation. This was 1969, in a Thai hospital, with my mom holding my hand, and I'm about to die. They did the first spinal tap, and squirted the fluid into a bucket; then, an hour later, the doctor returned. He spoke to my mother, and then she told me that the first tap hadn't worked, and that they're going to need to do it again. I, an ungodly sinner who didn't know Christ, crawled out of bed after the second procedure. I crawled over to my balcony, looked out below, and thought of dying. I was thinking: What am I going to do when I die? What happens? Where do I go? I was close to death, and God in His mercy and goodness healed me so that I could now preach and teach his healing power.

The Law of Faith

So, just what is faith? **Hebrews 11:1** gives us the only 100% accurate definition of faith.

Hebrews 11:1 says, "Now faith is the substance of things hoped for, the evidence of things not seen." The NIV states it this way: "Now faith is being sure of what we hope for, and certain of what we do not see."

So we see that faith has two elements- first, faith is being absolutely sure of what you're hoping for. Secondly, faith is being certain of what you don't see. In other words, faith involves being certain of the invisible.

- **Hebrews 11:6** "But without faith, it is impossible to please him; for he that cometh to God must believe that he is, and that he is a rewarder of them that diligently seek him."

Often, people say they need to have more of that faith. They say that the divine healing faith makes sense in their mind, but they ask for prayer to get more faith. I have something great to tell you- you don't need more faith, you just need to purify the faith you have. We see this in **Romans 12:3**, which says, "For I say, through the grace given unto me, to every man that is among you, not to think of himself more highly than he ought to think, but to think soberly, according as God has dealt to every man the measure of faith." Thus, you have faith; God has dealt it to you. This is also shown in the following passage:

- **Ephesians 2:8-9** "For by grace are you saved, through faith, and that not of yourselves. It is a gift of God."

Now, we go to **Mark 11:22.** Jesus had just cursed the fig tree. Peter said, "Wow! Lord, look the fig tree that you cursed. It withered from the roots." I love this detail about "withering up from the roots" because that is exactly how our mighty Jesus deals with problems. Men chop away at symptoms, and the outer branches of situations are diagnosed and treated. God dries things up from the roots! **Mark 11:22** says, "And Jesus answering unto them said, 'Have faith in God." He didn't say pray to get faith, or those of you that have faith should use it. He said "have faith" to all those who were listening. In the Greek, it can be rendered have the faith of God. When we look at the rest of the passage, this makes sense.

- **Mar 11:23** "For verily I say unto you, That **whosoever** shall say unto this mountain, 'Be thou removed, and be thou cast into the sea;' and shall not doubt in his heart, but shall believe that those

77

things which he saith shall come to pass, he shall
have **whatsoever** he saith."

Is healing included in the "whatsoever" Jesus mentioned
in this passage? It absolutely is! Jesus pointed to a literal
mountain and said, if you have faith as a grain of mustard
seed, you can say to this mountain, "Remove and cast into
the sea." That is one of the biggest things on the planet being
cast into one of the deepest things on the planet. If you can
do that, how much more can you move cancer out of your
body! Cancers are nothing to our great and mighty God. We
can see in **Ephesians 1** that cancer and every other disease
can be conquered by the authority of the believer in Christ.

- **Ephesians 1:15-23** "For this reason, ever since I
  heard about your faith in the Lord Jesus and your
  love for all the saints, I have not stopped giving
  thanks for you, remembering you in my prayers. I
  keep asking that the God of our Lord Jesus Christ,
  the glorious Father, may give you the spirit of
  wisdom and revelation, so that you may know
  Him better. I pray also that the eyes of your heart
  may be enlightened in order, that you may know
  the hope to which He has called you, the riches
  of His glorious inheritance in the saints, and His
  incomparable great power for us who believe.
  That power is like the working of His mighty
  strength, for which he exerted in Christ when he
  raised Him from the dead and seated Him at His
  right hand in the heavenly realms, far above any
  power and dominion and every title that can be
  given, not only in the present age, but also in the
  one to come. And God placed all things under his
  feet and appointed to be over everything in the
  church, which is his body, the fullness of Him

who fills everything in every way."

We continue to see this in **Ephesians 2: 4-6,** which says,

"God is so rich in mercy and he loved us, that even though we were dead because of our sins, he gave us life when He raised Christ from the dead. It is only by God's grace that you have been saved. For he raised us from the dead along with Christ, and seated us with Him in the heavenly realms, because we are united with Christ Jesus."

Where is our Savior, Christ Jesus right now? His Spirit is in our heart, but his physical body is far above all principalities, powers, dominions, and every name, and we are next to him. Are cancer, Alzheimer's, heart disease, and malfunctioning organs considered names? Of course the whole list of sicknesses, diseases, and other maladies are in the realm of named things and our Lord Jesus has the name that is above all those names!

When we get a grasp of the fact that we have the power that is above every name within us, sickness will no longer be a threat to you. We continue to see this in **Philippians 2:8-11:**

"And being found in fashion as a man, he humbled himself and became obedient to death, even death on a cross. Wherefore, God has highly exalted Him and given Him Jesus, a name that is above every name; that, at the name of Jesus, every knee should bow, of things in heaven, and things in the earth, and things under the earth, and that every tongue should confess that Jesus Christ is Lord to the glory of God the Father."

We now have seen the power which we have faith in, and how powerful that power is. We now go on to learn more about faith:

- **Hebrews 11:6** "But without faith it is impossible to please Him: for he that cometh to God must believe that He is, and that He is a rewarder of them that diligently seek Him."

Why is it impossible to please God without faith? This passage says it is because anyone who comes to Him must believe two things: first, that He exists, because if we didn't believe this we would not even start in our journey to commune with Him. Then, we must believe that He rewards those who earnestly seek Him. This is seen clearly in every revealed interaction between God and man in the Bible.

Also, today, in every interaction with men, God honors faith. Jesus never responded to earthly needs without at least a spark of faith being spoken or demonstrated. In the gospel accounts, we see the principle of faith being intertwined with prayer. Let us start with **Mark chapter 11**; the context is that Jesus had approached a fig tree, found no fruit on it to eat, and cursed it forever.

- **Mark 11:11** "And Jesus entered into Jerusalem and into the temple: and when he had looked round about upon all things, and now the eventide was come, he went out unto Bethany with the twelve."

- **Mark 11:12** "And on the morrow, when they were come from Bethany, he was hungry:"

- **Mark 11:13** "And seeing a fig tree afar off having leaves, he came, if haply he might find any thing thereon: and when he came to it, he found nothing but leaves; for the time of figs was not yet."

- **Mark 11:14** "And Jesus answered and said unto it, No man eat fruit of thee hereafter for ever. And his disciples heard it."

- **Mark 11:20** "And in the morning, as they passed by, they saw the fig tree dried up from the roots."

The next day, Jesus and His disciples passed by the cursed fig tree. Peter commented on how it had withered up from the roots.

- **Mark 11:21** "And Peter calling to remembrance saith unto him, Master, behold, the fig tree which thou cursedst is withered away."

Wouldn't this have been a great opportunity for Jesus to say something like, "You know Peter, I create trees and when there's no figs on them I also wither them *because I'm God.*" Although He could have said that, because Jesus was and is God, He didn't. Jesus used His faith in God, and then used the withered tree as a demonstration to teach us how to pray with the same faith that He did.

- **Mar 11:22** "And Jesus answering saith unto them, Have faith in God."

In **Matthew 21: 20-22** we see the same event from a different perspective. From the pen of Matthew, God says the same thing with additional emphasis.

- **Mat 21:20** "And when the disciples saw *it,* they marveled, saying, 'How soon is the fig tree withered away!'"

- **Mat 21:21** "Jesus answered and said unto them, 'Verily I say unto you, If ye have faith, and doubt not, ye shall not only do this which is done to the fig tree; but also if ye shall say unto this mountain, "Be thou removed, and be thou cast into the sea;" it shall be done.'"

- **Mat 21:22** "And all things, whatsoever ye shall ask in prayer, believing, ye shall receive."

When the disciples saw this, they were amazed! I would have been too, wouldn't you? These men had been learning from Jesus for some time. Yet they asked, "How did the fig tree wither so quickly?" We hear Jesus replying, "I tell you the truth, if you have faith and do not doubt, not only can you do what was done to the fig tree, but also you can say to this mountain, Go, throw yourself into the sea and it will be done. If you believe, you will receive whatever you ask for in prayer."

Now, let us not "spiritualize" Jesus' words in these passages. I can see Jesus pointing to a literal mountain range, when saying that we can also say to this mountain for it to be removed and be cast into the sea. Take confidence in the God who moves your mountains! Yes, speak and it shall be done and all things whatsoever you ask in prayer, believing, you shall receive! You can use this power of faith in your heart right now and release your healing by speaking what you believe into your body.

Mark 11:22-24 is one of the keys to a truly successful prayer life that God loves to answer. We can all have this faith in God, for Jesus commanded it. He tells us all that if anyone of us says to our mountain to go throw itself in to the sea, and does not doubt in his heart, but believes that what he says will happen, it will be done for us. Therefore, Jesus is telling us that whatever we ask for in prayer, we are to believe that we have received it, and it will be ours. Based upon **Hebrews 11:1**, is faith the same as hope? When Jesus said above that we are to believe that we received our healing, did he mean to hope that we did? If you answered no to those questions, you are correct according to the Scriptures. Why is faith not the same as hope? For this answer, we look in other biblical passages, and we see that God distinguishes between faith and hope. Even though they are related and occur together with meanings and purposes that are intertwined, they are not the same thing. For example, in **1st Corinthians 13:13** we read the following truth:

- **1Corinthians 13:13** "And now abideth faith, hope, charity, these three; but the greatest of these is charity."

If they were the same, God would not have separated them into three distinct concepts. Therefore, faith *is not* hope.

Faith is Not Hope

The reason some do not receive answers to their prayers is they are praying and hoping instead of praying in faith. It is not their fault. Over the years, we have often been taught to keep "praying and hoping." Praying and hoping is a good start. This is because if you do not have any hope, you will not bother to get on your knees and try to pray. If you do not have any hope, why even open your mouth? Hope gets you to your knees, but hope does not get you the answer to your prayers. Let's look again at what **Hebrews 11:1** tells us about what faith really is.

- **Heb 11:1** "Now faith is the substance of things hoped for, the evidence of things not seen."

You can see that faith is not hoping. Yes, faith is being sure and certain of our hopes. Faith is being sure of our hopes, and being certain of invisible realities.

Being sure of invisible realities is not hard. Let's start with this thought and see how easy it is to believe God in prayer like our Lord did. It's not hard to believe in the invisible. We do it all the time. When you close the refrigerator door, do you know what happens to the light inside? If you think it went off, how do you know? Don't tell me you've been in there! We really don't know by sensory perception what happens to the light in a refrigerator with the door closed. We take it by faith that it goes off, because, when we push the little button in the door with the door standing open, we experience repeatedly that the light goes off. Faith in invisible realities is also shown in our act of confidence when we drop a letter in the mailbox. Do you actually see the mailman come, open the mailbox, and take your letter to the post office?

Of course not; we just have faith. Any doubt about this process comes from experiences of the system failing us, and from hearing about other people's negative experiences with the post office. On the other hand, if all we ever heard is that the post office had never lost a piece of mail, and that they've always been on time, then we'd have a lot of faith in the postal system. But hearing or experiencing failures gives one doubt about the postal system. In the sphere of healing, we must get our eyes off of other people's experiences, and onto the God who wants to deliver His promises to us.

Here is another everyday example of how we believe in the reality of the invisible. On the way to work, some of you might have crossed a bridge or two. Sometimes bridges have signs that notify us of their maximum weight capacity. Perhaps the amount of tons or the number of vehicles measures the capacity. How many people have ever stopped their car and paced along the shoulder of the road anxious and worried trying to be sure whether or not their vehicle is under the weight limit? Just imagine being on the bridge with a big, heavy truck passing you. Have you ever started worrying about the bridge's weight limit being exceeded? No! On the contrary, in total faith, you drive right over that bridge. You see we use faith all the time. This is the same faith that heals even incurable diseases!

In conclusion, healing is easier. It is easier than what we have been told by men whose belief systems are based on the traditions or experiences of men. The prerequisite for pleasing God in prayer is to believe God. We do not get healed by our Father in prayer by just hoping, though hope is an important place to start. Hope is a foundation stone that faith builds upon. When we pray, we start with hoping, then we shift into believing the surety of our prayer, and we finally have a certainty about the invisible reality of our answer. In prayer for healing, your believing and receiving are present according to Jesus, our Great Physician!

Chapter Five-
Points of Contact
for Receiving Your Healing

—+—

Oral Roberts, one of the great men who taught and practiced faith in Christ for healing in recent times, rein-
forced with his audiences the concept of having "points
of contact" to receive healing from God. He showed that
throughout Christ's earthly ministry, He set a point of contact
whereby people could release their faith in Him. Many others
who have been mightily used by God in this century have
also demonstrated that a point of contact is something that
you do because you believe that Jesus is there and heals you
at that point and place in time. It is at that very moment that
you release your faith to God and receive your healing.

Using these points of contact is like turning on a light
switch. You expect the lights to come on every time you flip
the switch. Why? Well because you know that the switch is
connected to the Power Company. You never have to doubt
this process.

So countless thousands of those in search of healing
from "incurable diseases" through the years have used these
points of contact as starting points and have been wonder-
fully healed by Jesus!

Today, as you read this chapter, I am asking you to consider setting a day, time, and a specific faith action, either alone or with someone else who believes. Use one or more of the points of contact we will cover in this chapter or something new that springs from your faith creatively. (One Old Testament character, Namaan, actually dipped 7 times in the muddy Jordan River and by faith in the Word of the Lord, through the prophet Elijah, was healed of leprosy!) Yes, as we go through these points of contacting God for healing, remember something very important that the man of God, Lester Sumrall, shared in his book "Miracles Don't Just Happen." In this book, Brother Sumrall reminded us that Jesus taught in both word and by example that there is no pre-packaged routine for receiving one's healing. Jesus didn't anoint everyone with oil. He did not lay hands on everyone nor did he put mud on everyone's eyes, though these were all some of the many methods used at points in his ministry. With this variety, Jesus showed us that all healing is Divine regardless of the point of contact employed. There is no religious formula but it is through faith in the Name of Jesus that every person who believes in the Lord Jesus Christ can obtain his or her God given healing today!

Our prayer is that you will be encouraged to personally trust in the eternally reliability of the Word of God, and reach out to take the physical healing that Jesus Christ provided for you when He bore your sicknesses and carried your pains over 2000 years ago.

Finally, remember that in the body of Christ today, the ground is level at the foot of the cross. Yes, God does use and is using many anointed ministries in the gifts of healing, and wonderful healing ministers are here to help us. This we are not denying. However, the Good News in that you, as a child of God, can contact your Heavenly Father by your own faith through the same finished work of the Lord Jesus Christ's cross as can the most anointed man or woman of God!

What should I do if there are no results?

If there are no results after using these points of contact, then do a reality check. Ask yourself, is the message of Divine Healing simply thoughts in your mind, and not yet complete childlike faith from the depths of your heart? In other words, is what we have merely in the mind, and not of a fully persuaded heart full of childlike faith in the Word of God? Just believing that Jesus can heal you is not faith for healing. Now, don't get me wrong.

There is an element of "belief" in faith, but faith is more than belief. Yes, faith means we are as sure about the Word of God as we are about our own name. Now, don't misunderstand, faith is tested, and overcoming doubts is a part of being healed; but, when we do have faith, we will act accordingly without having to "work it up." There can also be emotions involved around faith, but some confuse faith with emotions, and this is also a big mistake. Emotions and desires are often mistaken for faith, and then it is too often that those who have failed to get healed blame God or His messengers.

If you have not had initial success just pause and start over. This time, believe that God is working His word in your mind, and working His healing in your body for His good pleasure.

- **Philippians 2:13** "For it is God who works in you both to will and to do for His good pleasure."

For me, the answer to my failures has been to go back to being like a child in my relationship with the Lord who heals us. I usually have made things too complicated. Remember when your father or someone you loved put you up on a ledge or a chair and held out their arms saying, "Go ahead and jump and I will catch you!" This is beautifully depicted in a passage in **Isaiah 27:5** which invites us to "Let him take hold of My strength."

I can just picture you reaching up to Jesus right now and taking hold of the Lord's hand and His strength! The very strength of God flows through your hands into the part of your body that needs His healing touch. Every time you need His help in maintaining your faith, you just reach up and grab the Lord's healing hands. Every time you think of it, lift your hands again, take hold of His strength, and thank Him for hearing you. When He heard you, He healed you! Right now receive more strength to endure as the symptoms leave your body to be replaced by Divine Health!

Pray your own prayers of faith

Jesus taught each one of us how to pray in faith. He said in **Mark 11:22-24**, that we should have faith in God or as the literal translation can be rendered, "have the very faith *of* God." He went on to say that when we pray, we should believe that we receive whatever we pray for, and then we shall have it. He gave us this faith to use, for we see in **Hebrews 12:2** that Jesus is the Author and Finisher of our Faith. God has given each of us "the measure of faith," as he says in **Romans 12:2**. You do have enough faith! Furthermore, this faith is imparted from the heart of God Himself to enable you to see and achieve the impossible! Jesus promised this to you in, **Mathew 17:20,** "If ye have faith as a grain of mustard seed, ye shall say unto this mountain, remove hence to yonder place; and it shall remove; and nothing shall be impossible unto you."

When you pray in faith, you pray according to what God wants, and therefore you know that God has given you your requests. There is no struggle in it. We are not trying to persuade God to heal us. By the way, this Divine Healing concept is His idea! He has said in **Psalms 103:1-3,** "Bless the Lord, O my soul: and all that is within me, bless his holy name. Bless the Lord, O my soul, and forget not all his bene- fits: Who forgiveth all thine iniquities; who healeth all thy diseases;"

Asking God to heal you of diseases, and believing that He heard you, is as easy as asking for him to forgive your sins and believing that He has forgiven you.

Faith for healing is a gift you have been given. We do not struggle to accept a gift. We trust that the person giving it to us has our best interest at heart. So, we accept with faith in that belief. Let the calm peace of God enter into your heart and mind. You have already received what God uses to heal. So, you have the faith to move both mountains and disease from your body!

Prayer of Agreement with other believers

Most of us have needed the encouragement and prayers of others to join us as we stand in faith for healing. Perhaps now would be a good time for you to swallow your pride and call a good friend to come pray with you for healing. Find someone who believes that it is still God's will to heal you today as the Word of God states.

Jesus taught us to pray jointly for the synergism, and effective strength we gain from it, in the presence of God our Father.

In **Matthew 18:18-20** He says, "Verily I say unto you: Whatsoever ye shall bind on earth shall be bound in heaven, and whatsoever ye shall loose on earth, shall be loosed in heaven. Again I say unto you, that if two of you shall agree on earth as touching any thing that they shall ask, it shall be done for them by my Father which is in heaven. For where two or three are gathered together in my name, there am I in the midst of them."

Of course, there is no rule here regarding what to say, Perhaps you can start a prayer similar to this prayer: "Lord, I want to be healed in order to more fully serve you without restrictions. We agree in the name of Jesus that you now heal me by all means, including natural, spiritual, and medical from _____. We agree that by Jesus' wounds we are healed, and thank you for this provision becoming our present possession right now, in Jesus' Name, on this day _____ at the time of _____ Amen. "

Remember this moment when your healing started. Keep a faith-image in your mind that your healing did begin. Writing this information down will help you remember and give you something to refer to when you begin to doubt. Try to remember the joy of it. You are going to hold on to your healing in Jesus' Name.

The anointing of oil by the elders

Church history clearly shows that for centuries, elders in the Christian faith have been praying with trusting expectation for the Lord Jesus to heal his people. God has used their prayers to heal even the gravest illnesses. This is a truth first taught by the Lord Jesus' own brother, the apostle James.

James 5:14-16. "Is any sick among you? Let him call for the elders of the church; and let them pray over him, anointing him with oil in the Name of the Lord. And the prayer of faith shall save the sick, and the Lord shall raise him up, and if he has committed sins, they shall be forgiven him. Confess your faults one to another, and pray one for another, that ye may be healed. The effectual fervent prayer of a righteous man availeth much."

Notice that the confession of our sins, as described in this passage, is a tremendous facilitator in the release of our faith for healing. The way to healing often begins with the open confession of faults to those we may have offended. It can also necessitate a public, heart felt honesty about your weaknesses. Sometimes we struggle to repent. If we do, at least we can cry out and ask God to make us willing to repent. It may sound something like this, "Dear Heavenly Father, is there any sin, attitude, habit, or neglect in my life? If so, please show me so I can repent and close the door. In Jesus' Name."

According to the Bible, calling for the elders is a direct command by God to all sick Christians. Yet, how many have done this, and how many elders would be prepared to pray in faith if they were called upon? What a shame that there is so much unbelief in today's churches. This is a sin for which we should repent.

Now, the sicknesses depicted in the passage in James sound to be severe, or even "incurable." They are not mild, occasional headaches that people are trying to get rid of. The very phrase, "The Lord will *raise him up*" depicts a severe and debilitating condition. The word **"raise,"** which is from the Greek **"egerei,"** means to raise up or lift up, just like Jesus did Peter's mother-in-law in **Mark 1:31**. It paints the picture that this individual may have been bedfast, terminally ill, or really down and out.

The anointing of the sick is not just for the original 12 apostles either. In **Mark 6:12-13** we read, "And they (the disciples) went out, and preached that men should repent. And they cast out many devils, and anointed with oil many that were sick, and healed them."

So just what should happen when the elders pray over us? First, any one calling for the elders must believe, as well as the godly men we call, that using their faith will administer healing.

In **Mark 9:17-27** we see where a poor father who brought his demon-possessed son to the Lord said, "If thou canst do anything, have compassion on us, and help us." Jesus replied, "If thou canst believe, all things are possible to him that believeth." In other words, Jesus is saying to us today: "The "if" does not lay with me, for of course, I can heal your son; but, you must exercise an expectant faith." Again, even Jesus, the Chief Shepherd, *could not* heal some because they would not believe." We see this situation in **Mark 6:1-6**: "He (Christ) could there do no mighty work, save that he laid his hands upon a few sick folk, and healed them. And he marveled because of their unbelief. And he went round about the villages teaching."

Matthew 13:58 states this from just a slightly different perspective. "And he (Christ) did not many mighty works there because of their unbelief."

Spoken commands of faith in the Name of Jesus.

On a recent trip to Kerela, a southwestern province of India, I had the privilege of sharing the Word of healing to a crowd of around 2,500 at a Divine Retreat Center. After sharing the good news that our Lord Jesus Christ desired to heal them, we were filled with compassion. There were so many in need of healing, so little space around the altar, and so little time to minister. What else could we do but speak the word of faith as those in need of healing laid hands on themselves. What a mighty God we serve! As in the days of old, our wonderful healing God saw their faith, and many received their healing by the touch of the Master! This is the day of the "latter rain," and our God is moving in healing power again just like in the book of Acts.

Acts 3: 7-9, with 3:16 and 4:9-10: In these passages we see how the apostle Peter used the spoken word of faith when the lame man was healed at the gate called Beautiful. When he said, "In the name of Jesus Christ of Nazereth, rise up and walk," his faith brought healing. He explained that it was faith in the name of Jesus that made him well. "His name, through faith in his name, has made this man strong, whom you see and know; the faith that is by him has given him perfect soundness in the presence of you all." When asked how this happened, Peter explained in **verse 9**, "If we this day be examined of the good deed done to this impotent sick man, by what means he has been made whole; be it known unto you all.....that by the name of Jesus Christ of Nazereth, whom ye crucified....even by him does this man stand here before you whole."

Peter declared that this miracle was performed directly by the Name of our Lord Jesus. Then again in **Acts 9:33-34**, Peter said to a man named Aeneas, who had been in bed eight years with the palsy, "Christ Jesus heals thee;" the man got out of bed, and began to serve the Lord Jesus who had healed him.

Right now, you can receive your healing by speaking to the diseased area or organ, and in Jesus Name, through faith in that all the power in His name, you will be healed.

Laying on of hands

Kathryn Kuhlman, who had a mighty anointing to bring Christ's healing because she understood Jesus promise in **Mark 16:17-18**, made the following wonderful quote in 1972: "There is no touch in the universe like the touch of Jesus' nail scarred hand. All who touch Him are made whole. All who touch Him discover salvation, healing, deliverance, and power. The Master's touch makes all things new."

- **Mark 16:17-18** "And these signs shall follow them that believe (literally this means "to those believ-

ing or the believing ones") in my name: they shall
cast out devils; they shall speak with new tongues;
They shall take up serpents, and if they drink any
deadly thing, it shall not hurt them; they shall lay
hands on the sick, and they shall recover."

This is a direct command, not merely a request from
Christ that his followers should pray for the sick by the
laying on of hands. We should go forth, and do so expecting
the sick to be healed by the Lord. Even a five-year-old can
do this. My children started practicing the laying on of hands
for healing with great results at about that age!

Oh, the power of the Master's touch when we stretch
forth our hands! Today, they are His hands, for we are the
body of Christ!

- **Mark 6:56** "As many as touched him were made
  whole."

Yes, even the soldiers who came to take Jesus, the minute
they reached to touch Him, all fell under His power in **John
18:6.** Then we see in **Mark 1:41,** the leper asked Jesus if he
would heal him, because he knew that Jesus could heal him.
Jesus touched the leper, and said, "I will, be thou clean," and
this settles forever the question of whether or not it is God's
will for you to be healed.

To those who contest the authenticity of the **Mark 16**
passage, it would be good for them to do an honest study of
Church history. They would see how in nearly every century
since the death of the apostles, that healing was preached
and practiced throughout the church. As for the authenticity
of the last verses in Mark's gospel, one of our early church
leaders, named Irenaeus, quotes this **Mark 16** passage
as "Mark's Gospel". By the way, Irenaeus was a pupil of
Polycarp, who in turn was a pupil of John the Apostle; so, I

think there is some apostolic authority behind this passage. (See Morrison's *Commentary on Mark* for more detail.)

Besides that, when healing is acted upon in faith, God honors his Word. This proves to us that God, who is faithful, not only is the author of healing, but backs it with the power of heaven! Go ahead and lay hands on yourself and others for healing. What do you have to lose?

Handkerchiefs and Aprons

Yes, the use of handkerchiefs or aprons as points of contact for healing actually does come from the Bible. In **Acts 19:11-12,** we see where, "God wrought special miracles by the hands of Paul: So that from his body were brought unto the sick handkerchiefs or aprons, and the diseases departed from them, and the evil spirits went out of them."

I realize that there have been abuses in this area. Some have actually had the audacity to sell little prayer cloths for profit on television. However, there is a tangible essence or tangibility of the Holy Spirit, which is actually transmitted by the anointing of cloths. Jesus had people touch the very hem of his garments, and he felt power flow out of him.

I have also prayed in faith over handkerchiefs, and then taken them to India to lay on the sick using that same faith. We have also given anointed cloths to ministers in India, and seen the blessings of God flow to and through them to their congregations. Of course, the healing is by the Holy Spirit, not by the cloths or the one who brings them. I would like to suggest that you pray over a handkerchief in faith, and put it under your pillow or somewhere on the body of a sick loved one. Remember the great promise of our Lord Jesus in **Matthew 17:20**, "If ye have faith as a grain of mustard seed, ye shall say unto this mountain, 'Remove hence to yonder place; and it shall remove; and nothing shall be impossible unto you."

In conclusion, there is no religious formula in these points of contact, but it is through faith in the Name of Jesus that every single believer in our Lord Jesus Christ can obtain their God given healing today!

Our prayer is that you have been encouraged to personally trust in the eternally reliable Word of God, and reach out to take the physical healing that Jesus Christ provided for you when he bore your sicknesses and carried your pains over 2,000 years ago!

Chapter Six-
Removing all Obstacles
to Your Healing

———+———

Testimony – of Ray Light.

In reading the testimony of a friend of mine, Ray Light, please notice how he removed obstacles to healing by praying to God in humility on his knees. He cried out for the Lord to "fix him" first and then saw the amazing, supernatural way God met him with healing from heart disease!

"My name is Ray Light. I was healed and am healed by God, that is, God the Holy Spirit through and in the name of Jesus.

Around July 19th, 1984, I was speaking to several people about how I did not feel good on this day. Most of these people had some kind of spiritual level about them. They told me I should seek my God for an answer or a deliverance to my situation.

So when I arrived at my residence, I go on my knees and asked God to help me. For the first time in my life I asked God to fix me of whatever was wrong with me and then I went to sleep. Sometime later, I believe in the wee hours of the evening as I slept, I began to have a great pain in my arms and chest.

Jesus, in this great soft light form, appeared to me. He was hovering above me. I was having a heart attack as I was sleeping. I was being pulled through a spinning tunnel millions or billions of miles long. Everything happened quickly, and without anything being said.

On my way through this spinning tunnel, the light of Jesus was continuously above me without any words being spoken. Then Jesus said, "Do you want to come with me?" Before I could answer, I had arrived at heaven's entry. I was suspended in a vast, beautiful blue entry to heaven, with Jesus' light hovering above me.

And then I said, "Yes, Lord I want to come with you, but I also want to stay." Jesus replied, "Because you said this, I will not allow you in". While I was at heaven's entry, basking in the peace, I was able to see hell below me. I could see the people's heads and foreheads that were in hell. Peace at my face, and yet below me the gnashing of teeth.

People speak of fire in hell, but I did not see flames. I believe flames are the pain and suffering that the Lord God permitted me to feel below me. God began sending me back, and healing my heart as I was coming back. I awoke with extreme pain in my chest and arms for a few seconds. The pain dissipated, and the light of Jesus faded away.

I was healed and am healed, thank you Jesus! The stripes on Jesus' back made my healing possible. Jehovah Rapha is the Healer and I thank Him! Seconds later I entered into the presence of the Holy Spirit. I believe for most of the night, I laid in bed feeling weightless, like I was levitating in mid air.

This was the most Divine or Supernatural healing I have ever had. But I have been healed and delivered of all kinds of vile and putrid attacks of all sorts my whole life.

My God is an awesome God! Please keep me in your mercy and grace, Jesus. I can not or could not live through the things that I have gone through without his mercy and grace. Jesus has shown me so much mercy and grace that sometimes I feel unworthy. Why me, and how much more can he give? Then I remember he is God; and why me, is because he loves me, that's why!

I still can not go another day without his grace, mercy, and goodness. Got a problem? Cry out to Jesus and He will hear you. Jesus is a relevant God for today's needs. Align your will so you can receive his goodness. Forgive if you can, and if you can not forgive, then ask Jesus to help you forgive. Ask Jesus to help you with anything you can or can not do. Ask until he does help you, for he wants to hear from you.

Align yourself with his Commandments, and your life should smooth out, though it probably won't be in your time or in your way. God can not lie, and he is a good God. Even when I feel beat up, chewed up, tore up, and beat down by life, my God is still a good God! He will always be there for me. Cry out to Jesus. My God will not allow us to have more than we can handle, for He is a good God. He created you and me, and He knows our limits. When you can not take anymore of anything, cry out to Jesus. The Holy Spirit will come in Jesus' name as you cry out to Jesus, as I did.

God sees your incredible potential, and you are the apple of His eye. God thinks you are fine, because you are his fine creation of every color, creed, and race."

Ray's testimony is a good example of how removed obstacles bring the free flow of God's healing power. Now, may the Lord show you also what obstacles may be blocking your healing as I present some of the most common obstructions that can keep healing from being a reality in people's lives.

Unrepented Sin:

John 5:14 In this verse, Jesus said to the man healed at the pool of Bethesda: "See you are well again. Stop sinning or something worse may happen to you.'" Both John the Baptist and Jesus' message, as you can see in **Matthew**

3:2,8,11, and 4:17, was "Repent, for the Kingdom of heaven is near." There, he was speaking to the Pharisees, and saying that the Kingdom of Heaven was very near them, but not in them, because they wouldn't change their mind. So, if you have any unrepented sin, God wants us to rethink and then redirect our lives. Pray a prayer like this one, which is found in **Psalm 18:28:** "Oh Lord, light my candle; enlighten my darkness." **Proverbs 20:27** says that the spirit of a man is the candle of the Lord searching the inward parts of your belly. **Psalm 139:23-24** urges us to cry out like David saying, "Oh Lord, search me; know my heart. Test me, know my thoughts. See if there is any wicked way in me, and lead me in the path of everlasting life."

We need to get to the point where we realize that **Psalm 19: 11-14** is true, which says, "Who can understand his own errors? Cleanse me God from my secret faults. Let the words of my mouth and the motives of my heart be acceptable in your sight." You see, if I know there is sin in my heart, and am not dealing with it, the Lord will not hear me. **Psalm. 66:18** The Lord's hand is not short that he can't heal you, and his ears are not dull that he can't hear you, but your iniquities have formed a gap between you and the Lord. Only one thing can bridge over that- when you confess your sins, Christ reconnects you to the Father, and the Holy Spirit then rushes in to do whatever you need.

Pride:

Matthew 5:3 "Blessed are the poor in spirit for theirs is the Kingdom of Heaven." When Christ pours out overflowing blessing onto us, it is easy for pride to creep in. We need to remember that what does a man have apart from God? No one has anything that God has not given them, including the breath we breathe. If we have a haughty spirit, it will prevent healing. Jesus said that blessed are the poor in spirit. He also said in **Matthew 5:6** - "Blessed are those who hunger and thirst for righteousness, for they will be filled." We are currently a product of how much we hungered for God yesterday, or a year ago. Whatever we are hungry for, we will be filled with, including whether it is just the status quo, sickness, or healing.

Anger:

Jesus said in **Matthew 5:22**, "Anyone who is angry with his brother will be subject to judgment. Anyone who says 'You fool!' will be in danger of the fire of hell." Snakes have a sac that they put their poison in so that they don't kill themselves; but, where are our sacs? We don't have them, for we have venom under our tongues according to God in **James 3**. So, when you become angry, the venom of your anger circulates throughout your body, reaching the edges of every extremity. Years of study in the field of medicine have proven that anger contributes to high blood pressure and can cause heart disease; thus, working hard to stay calm in every situation and not exploding in anger clears your path to healing power.

Lust:

Matthew 5:28 "Anyone who looks at a woman lustfully has committed adultery with her in his heart." Now, in order to combat our putrefying, perverted society, I suggest you do what Job did in **Job 31:1**, which says, "I made a covenant with my eyes. I will not lust on a young woman." This also applies to the reverse in gender, with women lusting for men. When you turn the bend in your car and see the suggestive billboard, open up a magazine and there's an advertisement with sexual implications, or you turn on the television and there is a raunchy commercial, you must take command over your eyes. Job said, "Eyes, I make a covenant with you. You will not look at those images." A great book, by an author I respect highly, Stephen Aterburn is <u>Every Man's Battle</u>. There is also a version for women, and every age. The book teaches you how to do "the bounce." You see, you can't keep the images from bombarding you, men. I speak to us because we are so visually oriented. When you see the unwholesome image, practice **Job 31:1**, and act like the image is a basketball- bounce your eyes off of it. You gravitate toward a lifestyle of what you envision and meditate upon. If you want the Holy Spirit to give you holy healing, you can't think, talk, walk, live, or breathe anything other than holiness. You can't have the Holy Spirit flowing through you in power if you have unholy thoughts. Yes, I know of men of God who had the power of the Holy Spirit strongly upon them, but were caught in adultery, alcohol, drugs, or any other evil. At some point, the Holy Spirit left, and a wrong spirit came in.

Apples come from apple trees, and oranges come from orange trees, just like the Holy Spirit within you yields holy gifts, holy anointing, and blessings to the Holy One. But, if you have sin within you, it will block healings.

Unforgiveness:

Matthew 6:14-15 "For if you do not forgive men their sins, your father will not forgive your sins." If you are being not forgiven because you are not forgiving, you can pray until you are blue in the face, but your healing won't come.

Judgmental Attitudes:

Matthew 7:1 "Do not judge, or you too will be judged." That has been misquoted many times, but what I do know is that the Lord wants us to heal the wounded Christian soldiers. We are the only army who kills it's wounded soldiers; we do so by excluding some in our faith through judgmental attitudes. We need to reach out with mercy to those in need, because at the time of judgment, mercy will prevail. If you gave mercy, you will be shown it by the Father. Pray, "Lord change me. Make me a different person in this situation, and with this person."

Impatience and Discouragement:

Matthew 7:7-11 "Ask (and keep on asking), Seek (and keep on seeking), Knock (and keep on knocking)." The action described here is a continuous process. You don't just knock and walk away form a door without waiting for them to have time to answer and help you with what you need.

Galatians 6:7-9 speaks of the Law of Sowing and Reaping. "Do not be deceived; God is not mocked. For whatsoever a man soweth, thus shall he reap. He that sows to the flesh shall from the flesh reap corruption; he that sows to the Spirit will from the Spirit reap life everlasting. Let us not become weary in doing good, for at the proper time we will reap a harvest, if we do not give up." Maybe you did receive your healing, but symptoms lingered or got worse, so you have given up. Change your mind about this and return to belief.

Self-life:

People sometimes say, "Heal me, heal me; but, I want to do what I want in my life. But, please heal me, heal me!" In **Matthew 8:21**, a man said, "Lord, let me first go and bury my father." "But Jesus told him, 'Follow me, and let the dead bury their own dead.'" In other words, Jesus said, "Follow me." When we get healed, we must follow the Master. We do not get healed and healthy to go out and do our own thing. God knows what we are going to do once we are healed, so we must have self-honesty as well as honesty to others.

Fear:

Matthew 8:23-27 This passage refers to the disciples out in the storm with their boat nearly sinking. They said, "Lord save us! We are going to drown!" Jesus replied, "You of little faith, why are you so afraid?" Then Jesus got up, rebuked winds and waves and it was completely calm. This shows that fear and faith are two opposing forces. When people let symptoms administer fear to them after they have prayed for their healing, then you begin to say, think, and believe things that are against faith in the unchangeable, immutable, faithful God.

God has not given you a spirit of fear or timidity about your symptoms; he has given you power, love, and a sound mind. His power is like dynamite! It will blow fear out of your life. **1 John 4:18** says, "There is no fear in love. But perfect love drives out fear, because fear has to do with punishment, and the one who fears is not perfected in love." You know that he loves you, and you know that he wouldn't have allowed the symptoms to come upon you without you having enough faith to overcome it; for, in **1 Corinthians 10:13**, we see that you are able to deal with everything that comes your way, whether it's physical, financial, marital, domestic, mental, psychological, relational. It says, "No temptation has seized you except what is common to man, and God is faithful. He will not let you be tempted beyond what you can bear. But when you are tempted, he will also provide a way out, so that you can stand up under it." The level of your testing is a measurement of God's confidence in your faith. So, you are above everything that comes your way.

We know that symptoms minister fear instead of helping our faith. However, in my thirty years of Divine Health, I choose not to believe the natural symptoms over the indisputable Word of God. We have read of Abraham in **Romans 4** and can see that it was a reality in the natural realm that he and Sarah were too old to have children. So, when we admit we feel pain, it is real, and we do not deny it. We must decide if we are going to live by the natural realities, or by a superior, sovereign, controlling reality called the Word of God, which brought the natural reality into existence, and is greater than the natural. We are not denying the reality of symptoms, but if you believe the symptoms, you will live in fear. If you listen to the God of Heaven who brought you into existence, and sent his Son to bear our pain, sickness, and disease by his wounds, you will have no fear.

The religious "crowds:"

Mark 5:25-35 With the healing of the woman with the issue of blood, three times it is said that there were crowds or great crowds surrounding Jesus. (**See vs. 27, 30, 31**) This woman had to press through the crowds, even though she had a condition of bleeding. Because she was viewed by society to be unclean, she was forbidden to do this by the religious teachings of the day. Just as the crowds did not allow her access to Jesus, some religious crowds say healing is not for today. But she did come to Jesus for healing, because she had heard of Jesus and this brought faith for her healing. Then she said, "if I may but touch the hem of his garment I will be made whole." She pressed her way through the crowds, and reached down or crawled under the crowds to take her healing.

Notice Jesus said that her faith made her whole. How do we know that this woman had faith to be healed?

She kept repeating "if I can touch him" over and over again. She had heard a testimony, and believed in her heart of hearts that Jesus had the power to heal. The woman took her healing. **Faith**: Her action was coming and then touching; **Fact**: the blood was dried. It was after she had faith and after she was healed that she then **Felt**. Look carefully at the process of her healing, for it is the same process that heals you!

Looking at the vessel or stumbling over the people God uses:

Matthew 10:40-41- "He who receives you receives me, and he who receives me receives the one who sent me. Anyone who receives a prophet, because he is a prophet, will receive a prophet's reward." You can receive healing through a vessel of any age if you believe; for it is written, "out of the mouth of babes and sucklings I have ordained strength." Young Josiah, a King of Israel, was eight years old when he began to rule; he opened up the word of God, got it in his heart, and a revival broke out among the nation. Thus, you get what you perceive and believe is coming through a person. If you don't believe God is using people to heal through even today, then it stops this blessing to you. We see this in **Matthew 10: 40-41**, "He who receives you (he said to his disciples) receives me, and he who receives me receives the one who sent me."

Resisting the Holy Spirit:

You can't resist the Holy Spirit's urgings, nudging, and convictions twenty three hours of the day, and then expect to be healed when you ask him for something in the other hour. **In Matthew 12:28**, it says, "If I drive out demons by the Spirit of God, then the Kingdom of God has come upon you." Jesus drove out demons and healed by the power of the Spirit of God; when the Spirit of God moved, the Kingdom was there. In other words, the Spirit of God has set the gifts of healings in the church. **1 Corinthians 12:9**- "The Spirit has given gifts of healing." **Romans 8:11**- "If the Spirit of Him who raised Jesus from the dead is living in you, he who raised Christ from the dead will also give life to your mortal bodies through his Spirit who lives in you." This "giving of life by the Spirit" is not just speaking of the resurrection, or the Greek word would be **"nekros."** It is the Spirit who now gives life to our physical body today, and this is shown by the use of the Greek word **"thnetos"** here.

The bottom line here is that if you resist the Holy Spirit most of your day, you can't go to a Divine Healing meeting for an hour and expect to say yes to him for healing. As we saw in **Mark 16:15-20**, if the Spirit of God lives in you, then you can lay hands on your own body and speak healing. However, you can't resist the Holy Spirit on one hand and expect him to heal through your other.

Falling away from the Word over trouble and persecution:

Matthew 13: 20-21- Some people "receive the word with joy." Then when trouble or persecution comes, the root of their faith is too shallow to support the stem, and they fall away. Since they have no root, their faith lasts only a short time, for when trouble or persecution comes because of the Word, they quickly fall away.

This speaks of the classic example of the seed falling into shallow ground. For example, You go home with great faith in your healing, but then someone you love and trust says, "I'm going to have the pastor talk to you, because healing is not for today." Learn to expect, but not allow this kind of attack on your faith, even from well meaning people. Love them, but refuse the spirit of unbelief.

Worries and the deceitfulness of wealth:

Matthew 13:22-23- Some people "hear the Word, but the worries of this life and the deceitfulness of wealth choke it, making it unfruitful." The worries of the world choke out the Word in many lives today. We get so busy working, driving the kids around to activities, and even going to church activities that we have no time to spend with the Lord on our own. Perhaps life has become so good we don't think we need God anymore. After all, we have money and all it can buy, so why bother with church, the Word, or prayer. Now, having money is not wrong if used for the right reasons. However, if the only time you can enjoy that new boat is on Sunday mornings, then it possesses you instead of you possessing it. All of these things can keep people from holding on to their healing.

Unbelief:

Matthew 13:54-57- People in Jesus' hometown asked, "Where did he get this power?" Familiarity with him and his family caused unbelief. "He did not do many miracles there because of their lack of faith." The King James Version says, "...because of their unbelief." There can be a "community of unbelief" around you. A community of unbelief produces a life of unbelief. In this verse, we see that even Jesus could not do any might work, because people were familiar with him and would not believe. Learn to love the people in the community, but not the spirit of unbelief.

Traditions of men:

Matthew 15:3,6,9- "Jesus asked, 'Why do you break the command of God for the sake of your tradition?' He said, 'Thus you nullify the word of God for the sake of your traditions. They worship me in vain: their teachings are but rules taught by men.'" Today, there is a tradition of men stating that healing and miracles ceased in the first century. However, it is intellectually unfaithful to tell someone that, because they can go right to the library, like I did, and search through church history and find that indeed healing and miracles have never ceased; and apostles are here today, planted within the church, to help people around them.

Demonic Oppression:

Jesus rebuked demons, they came out of the people, and they were healed. Now, think, if a doctor prescribes a medicine, and that medicine causes the root problem of the sickness to leave, the person is healed. Jesus cast out a demon from the boy in **Matthew 17 :18-21,** and the boy was healed. What does that show? That the demon was causing the sickness in the boy. The verses say, "Jesus rebuked the demon and it came out of the boy, and he was healed from that moment." Then he said, "But this kind does not go out except by prayer and fasting." See also **Luke 4:38-39**, where Jesus rebuked a fever, "and it left her"; we also see this in **Luke 13:10-17**, where a woman had a "spirit of infirmity" for 18 years; Jesus said Satan had bound her and he loosed her from this oppression in order to heal her. You as a born again child of God also have the authority to cast out any spirit causing sickness in the name of our Mighty Lord Jesus! As mentioned in Chapter 2, in Chicago I was ministering in a small Indian church where they speak Malayalam. A beautiful little girl about 8 years old came forward with her parents. The pastor told me she had been diagnosed with asthma. I felt electricity coming through my arm into my hand. The Lord said "cast it out." I spoke to the asthma, and commanded it to leave the little girl in the name of Jesus. Later, I received a phone call stating that the parents had taken their daughter back to the doctor and he could find no trace of asthma in her. Glory to God that when we use the authority in Jesus Name, Satan has to pack up his bags and go! Cancer is also often a demon spirit. One night my family was having dinner with a couple we know, and the husband had cancer. God had shown me that it was a demon, but the man came from a church that did not believe in divine healing. On this night, with his permission, our whole family encircled him and holding hands we prayed. I commanded the spirit of cancer to leave him. Afterward, week after week the blood tests showed the "cancer markers" in the blood were going lower and lower. Finally, the cancer was gone completely and remains so five years later! What a mighty Jesus we serve!

My point is this, don't look for a demon behind every illness, but when God directs you, be faithful, resist the devil, and he will flee.

Another area of demonic oppression is that people today are inadvertently involved in cults and the occult. Occult would be such things as Harry Potter, Tarot cards, magic, and reading the horoscope. Through these activities, you enter Satan's camp and allow these evil spirits to oppress your life. There are multi generational curses on people who have been involved in the occult and in false religious cults. I would encourage you to sit down with pen and paper and ask the Lord to show you what it is you have done along these lines to offend God. Then denounce it as sin, ask forgiveness for it, including all the demonic forces involved, and walk away from these activities forever.

Unhealthy diets and habits:

1 Corinthians 6:13, 19-20 -"Food for the stomach and the stomach for food, but God will destroy them both." "The body is not meant for sexual immorality but for the Lord and the Lord for the body. Do you not know that your body is a temple of the Holy Spirit who is in you, whom you have received from God? You are not your own...you were bought at a price, therefore honor God with you body."

We believe that the items we purchase such as our home, cars, and computers and such are worth the price we pay for them. Jesus also believes that about us, because he paid a very high price for each one of us. Remember that you are worth the price that was paid for you. That price was the Blood of Jesus!

As His holy temple, we must learn how to eat healthy, take naps, and rest our bodies. Exercise is important in whatever form you enjoy or can do. Perhaps it would benefit you to take natural supplements. Cut back or give up things like alcohol, caffeine and sugar. You need to do these things so your temple will be strong and healthy. Since we do reap what we sow, we can't expect God to heal us if we won't do our part with exercise, diet, and rest. In this area, it is important to first see your doctor and the counsel of professionals in each field before taking action.

Chapter Seven-
Answers to 10 Divine
Healing Objections

---+---

Objection #1 -

It is not always God's will to heal my friend or family
member, because someone else you knew was prayed
for and they got worse or perhaps even died. By doing
this, you are judging God's will for healing based on other
people's failures. We should never base our theology or faith
on experience. What is the only basis for faith? God and his
word, for as **Romans 10:17** says, faith comes by hearing the
Word. We don't base our view of God's will for healing on
other people's experiences any more than we would base our
salvation on another person's success or failure as a Christian.
There are people who accepted Christ, confessed it, and were
baptized and are backslidden and living for Satan. Does that
shake us up about our faith in Christ? Absolutely not one
bit! Also, when salvation is preached, does every lost person
come to receive it? No. Does that mean that there's something wrong with the message, or that it doesn't work? Of
course not. Now, start connecting the dots to connect these
principles about salvation to healing. It's the same thing!
Believe in your heart that by the wounds of Christ you are

healed, and confess Him as your Healer, and you will be healed. Then, you still have symptoms and start to feel like you're not healed. Well, how many times have you felt un-annointed or like a terrible sinner! When you sin, you sometimes kind of wonder where you are with God, because you don't feel good after fighting with your spouse or getting in the flesh. But, we don't walk by how we "feel" or by sight, but by faith. This goes both for salvation and healing.

Just as in our faith for being forgiven of sin, we must each have personal faith in Christ to be healed. Looking at **Mark 9: 17-27,** we see a poor father who brought his demon-possessed son to the Lord and said, "'If thou canst do anything, have compassion on us, and help us.' Jesus replied, 'If thou canst believe, all things are possible to him that believeth.'" In other words, Jesus is saying to us today, I can do all things, including healing, if you will believe in me. The word "if" in this passage belongs to us not to Christ. He is capable and will heal if we have faith.

Matthew 13:58 states, "And he (Christ) did not many mighty works there because of their unbelief." Unbelief stops healing, whether it is the unbelief of the recipient, or of another who prays for the person. This is also shown in **Mark 6:1-6,** where we see that "he (Christ) could there do no mighty work, save that he laid his hands upon a few sick folk, and healed them. And he marveled because of their unbelief. And he went round about the villages teaching."

Only praying "God please be with my friend or family member in their time of sickness" will not bring healing. This is a very religious sounding prayer, and comes from sweet, well meaning Christians. However, asking God to "be with the sick" is like asking God to give us oxygen! Oxygen is already all around us and so is God's abiding presence! In **Hebrews 13:15,** He has promised never to leave us nor forsake. So, why are people not healed when they ask for him to be with them? They are not healed because they don't ask for healing with the belief that He hears and grants their petitions in spite of your feelings or symptoms.

- **James 4:2** says, "Ye lust, and have not: ye kill, and desire to have, and cannot obtain: ye fight and war, yet ye have not, because ye ask not."

- **Mark 11:24** says, "Therefore I say unto you, 'What things so ever ye desire, when ye pray, believe, that ye receive them, and ye shall have them.'"

If you desire healing, then ask for healing, not just the presence of God! Just praying, "God give comfort to my friend and their family so they can get through this sickness" will not bring healing. God does give us comfort in and through our trials. As we see in **2 Corinthians 1:3-4,** "Blessed be God, even the Father of our Lord Jesus Christ, the Father of mercies, and the God of all comfort; who comforteth us in all our tribulation, that we may be able to comfort them which are in any trouble, by the comfort wherewith we ourselves are comforted of God."

If you only pray for comfort in sickness, don't complain if that is all you receive. Certainly, do not say that God does not or will not heal you. While comfort in sickness is one of His gifts, why not be clear about it if you are seeking healing? Why just ask only for comfort in sickness, when God gave Jesus' back to the whipping post in order to remove sickness in its entirely?

We can look at **James 5:13-16** for clear instructions on receiving more than just comfort! It says, "Is any among you afflicted? Let him pray. Is any merry? Let him sing psalms. Is any sick among you? Let him call for the elders of the church; and let them pray over him, anointing him with oil in the name of the Lord: And the prayer of faith shall save

(Greek-from "**sozo**", includes "**healing**") and the Lord shall raise him up; and if he have committed sins, they shall be forgiven him. Confess your faults one to another, and pray one for another, that ye may be healed. The effectual fervent prayer of a righteous man availeth much."

Only praying, "God teach us whatever lessons you are trying to teach us" will not bring healing. Do you as parents use sickness to teach your children? If so, we need to call the Department of Children and Family Services and report you as an unfit parent! **Matthew 7:7-11** "If ye then, being evil, know how to give good gifts unto your children, how much more shall your Father, which is in heaven, give good things to him that ask Him?"

Sickness is not a good thing. If we consider it a good thing, then why do we all try to avoid it and use every means at our disposal to get rid of it? We certainly are not being "good students" if God is trying to teach us something. Always remember:

- **James 1:17** "Every good gift is from above, and cometh down from the Father of lights, with whom is no variableness, neither shadow of turning."

No "variableness" means that God does not even change ever so slightly. God is not giving this sickness or tragedy to you and your family; God does not teach his children or increase their character by making them sick or sending them early death.

Objection #2 -

Sickness is for the glory of God. Those who hold to this fallacy often use **John 11:4** where Jesus said, "This sickness (of Lazarus) is not unto death, but for the glory of God, that the Son of God might be glorified thereby." In **John 11:1-46**

we see that God received no glory from Lazarus' sickness. No one expressed any pleasure in God, gave him credit or recognition until **verses 44-45** where we read:

- **John 11: 44-45**. " And he that was dead come forth, bound hand and foot with grave clothes; and his face was bound about with a napkin. Jesus saith unto them, Loose him, and let him go. Then many of the Jews, which came to Mary, and had seen the things which Jesus did, believed on him."

When did people believe on Jesus, before or after Lazarus was raised from the dead? Only after the miracle that included healing did God receive any glory! Common sense tells us that if God really gets glory from our sicknesses, then we should never attempt to get well. We are being dishonest by saying that God sends sickness to glorify himself or to do some good in our lives if we go to a medical facility in order to get treatment of the sickness! If we really want to be pious, why not pray for a "double portion" and for all of our children to get sick so our whole family will glorify God! This is nonsense, and those who take such a position are being hypocritical to seek any relief or cure by either prayer or medical attention.

Another passage used to support this error is **John 9:1-3**, which reads, "And as Jesus passed by, he saw a man which was blind from his birth. And his disciples asked him, saying, 'Master, who did sin, this man, or his parents, that he was born blind?' Jesus answered, 'Neither hath this man sinned, nor his parents; but that the works of God should be made manifest in him.'"

Now, if you just stopped there it may imply that the blindness was "the work of God being made manifest in him" (the blind man). But let us read on to **John 9:4 and 6,** which say,

- **John 9:4,6, "I must work the works of him that sent me,** while it is day: the night cometh, when no man can work." *So,* here we see that the works of God had not yet been done in the man who was born blind! "When he had thus spoken, he spat on the ground, and made clay of the spittle, and he anointed the eyes of the blind man with the clay. And said unto him, go wash in the pool of Siloam, which is by interpretation, sent. He went his way therefore, and washed, and came seeing."

- **John 9:24** In this verse the Pharisees say, "Give God the Praise: we know that this man is a sinner."

- **John 9:32** Here we have the blind man saying, "Since the world began, was it not heard that any man opened the eyes of one that was born blind."

So we see that the Bible clearly shows us that the healing of our bodies, not being sick or diseased or blind, gives God praise and glory!

Objection #3 -

Paul's thorn in the flesh- One tradition that has been well taught is referred to as "Paul's thorn in the flesh" from **2 Corinthians 12**. Everybody has heard about it. Really, it was not Paul's thorn, it was Satan's thorn. Tradition teaches that the thorn in the flesh was sickness or disease, but the Word plainly says that the thorn was a "messenger of Satan." Paul is writing this passage narrator style about himself:

120

- **2 Corinthians 12:1-7** "I knew a man in Christ above fourteen years ago (whether in the body, I cannot tell; or whether out of the body, I cannot tell: God knoweth) such as one caught up to the third heaven."

The three levels of heaven spoken about here are: first, the atmosphere, where planes fly. The second is the demon's realm, and the third is at the throne of God. That third heaven is where Paul went for a revelation from the Lord!

- **2 Corinthians 12:1-7 cont.** "And I knew such a man, (whether in the body or out of it, I cannot tell: God knoweth;) how that he was caught up into paradise, and heard unspeakable words, which it is not lawful for a man to utter. Of such an one will I glory: yet of myself I will not glory, but in mine infirmities. For though I would desire to glory, I shall not be a fool; for I will say the truth: but now I forebear, lest any man should think of me above that which he seeth me to be, or that he heareth of me. And lest I should be exalted above measure through the abundance of the revelations, there was given to me a thorn in the flesh, the messenger of Satan to buffet me, lest I should be exalted above measure."

Here we see the purpose of the thorn in the flesh: the thorn was given to buffet Paul

And, moreover, we are clearly given what the thorn was- a messenger of Satan to repeatedly hit Paul. This Greek word is translated as "messenger" 7 times in the New Testament. It is translated "angel" 181 times in the New Testament. All 188 times it is speaking of a personality and not a thing like a sickness or disease. Sickness is not a messenger. It is not a personality, but the word messenger is a "personality." It was an angel or a messenger of Satan assigned to Paul to buffet him. The word buffet means "to give repeated blows, over and over, and over." Weymouth's translation says, **2 Corinthians 12:8**- "Concerning this, three times have I besought the Lord, that he might leave me." The KJV says, "For this thing I besought the Lord thrice, that it might depart from me."

The thorn in the flesh was not a sickness as tradition teaches, but a messenger from Satan as the Bible teaches. God does not use Satan's messenger service. God did not give Paul this thorn in the flesh, but Satan sent Paul the "thorn" to stop the Word from being preached.

In the following verses we see an example of how Satan buffeted Paul:

- **Acts 13:45** "But when the Jews saw the multitudes, they were filled with envy, and spake against those things which were spoken by Paul, contradicting and blaspheming."

- **Acts 13:50** "But the Jews stirred up the devout and honorable women, and the chief men of the city, and raised persecution against Paul and Barnabas, and expelled them out their coasts."

- **Acts 14:5-6** "And when there was an assault made both of the Gentiles and also of the Jews with their **rulers, to use *them* despitefully and to stone them, they were aware of it, and fled unto Lystra and Derbe.**"

- **Acts 14:19-20** "And there came thither certain Jews from Antioch and Iconium, who persuaded the people, and having stoned Paul, drew him out of the city, supposing he had been dead. Howbeit, as the disciples stood round about him, he rose-up, and come into the city: and the next day he departed with Barnabas to Derbe."

In every place, the messenger of Satan stirred up perse-cution and affliction against Paul- blow by blow, buffet after buffet. Everywhere he went, there was trouble and persecution. The terms "thorn in the flesh" or "thorn in the side" are always used as an illustration in the Bible. For example, the Lord told Moses that if the Israelites did not drive out the inhabitants of the land of Canaan, those inhabitants would be "pricks in their eyes and thorns in their sides" (**Numbers 33:55.**)

Tradition says this thorn in the flesh was something in Paul's flesh; The Canaanites were not sticking into the Israelites sides! This is just an illustration. Today, we still use the term "a thorn in the flesh;" Your neighbor might be a "thorn in our side". In the same way we say, "that guy is a pain in the neck". It is the same type of illustration.

Weymouth's translation says, "There was given me a thorn in the flesh, Satan's angel to torture me" **2 Corinthians 12:7**. This evil sprit was assigned to Paul in order to stop the Word. Jesus said in **Mark 4** that Satan comes immediately to steal the Word. Paul had to stand against this evil spirit everywhere he went. Satan came to buffet Paul because of the abundance of revelations he received about the authority of the believer. Paul sought the Lord three times that he might be rid of him. It is useless to ask God to get rid of the devil for you. Paul had authority over Satan; it was up to him to use that authority. The Bible says, "Resist the devil, and he will flee from you," in **James 4:7**. God won't resist the devil for you. You have to do it yourself. If you don't cast the devil out, you will just have to live with him or get somebody else to help you cast him out.

When Paul asked God to do something about the messenger of Satan, the Lord said, "My grace is sufficient for thee." **2 Corinthians 12:9.** Tradition says that he asked the Lord to deliver him, and the Lord said no. So, Paul had to endure the thorn forever. The Bible actually says, "and he said unto me, my grace is sufficient for thee: for my strength is made perfect in weakness." God was saying, "My favor is enough. You have authority .You have the name of Jesus, and when you are humanly weak, my strength or my power is made perfect."

You can see how helpless we have been with traditions planted in our hearts and minds instead of God's Word. You cannot stand in faith against sickness and disease when you have been taught that sickness is God's will for you. How can you stand in faith when you think God has put cancer on you to teach you something? This irrational thinking is an abomination to the nature of God! How can you say that a loving God would put sickness on you to teach you something? If you believe that, then you need to quit taking your medication; if it is God's will for you to be sick, then to take medicine would be to fight against the will of God.

Objection #4 -

What about Epaphroditis, Timothy and Trophimus?
Philippians 2:25-30 tells us about Epaphroditis:

- **Vs. 25** "Yet I supposed it necessary to send to you Epaphroditus, my brother, and companion in labor, and fellow soldier, but your messenger, and he that ministered to my wants."

- **Vs. 26** "For he longed after you all, and was full of heaviness, because that ye had heard that he had been sick. "

- **Vs. 27** "For indeed he was sick nigh unto death: but God had mercy on him; and not on him only, but on me also, lest I should have sorrow upon sorrow."

- **Vs. 28** "I sent him therefore the more carefully, that, when ye see him again, ye may rejoice, and that I may be the less sorrowful."

- **Vs. 29** "Receive him therefore in the Lord with all gladness; and hold such in reputation:"

- **Vs. 30** Because for the work of Christ he was nigh unto death, not regarding his life, to supply your lack of service toward me."

The term, "not regarding his life, to supply your lack of service toward me." implies that Epaphroditus was burning the candle at both ends, probably working long hours and taking unnecessary risks doing the Lord's work. We must listen to the Lord regarding sufficient sleep and risk taking.

We see here what the Bible says about **Timothy**:

- **1 Timothy 5:23** "Drink no longer water, but use a little wine for thy stomach's sake and thine often infirmities."

God expects us to use common sense regarding our diet. For example, when you are in a country that has food or water that is not healthy for you, then God expects you not to drink or eat it. To do otherwise, unless there is no other alternative, would be irresponsible, even if you pray over it. Timothy wouldn't have had stomach problems if he had not drunk the bad water. So, he quit drinking the water and drank a little wine instead, and all was well.

What about **Trophimus**? **2 Timothy 4:20** says, "Trophimus have I left at Miletum sick."

This passage simply says that Paul left a man sick. So what? It does not tell us why. Nothing more is said regarding Trophimus, other than he is from Ephesus. (See **Acts 21:29.**).

When we study Jesus' healing ministry, we see that even Jesus did not always heal everyone. This was because of **unbelief**, not that it was not his will. **Mark 6:1-6** "He could do no mighty work except he laid hands on a few sick folk."

Again, we do not know why Trophimus was left in Miletum sick. But, it points out the fact that we can't have faith for another adult. However, our faith can agree with their faith. To see how Paul practiced this, see:

- **Acts 14:8** "There sat a certain man at Lystra, impotent in his feet, being a cripple from his mother's womb, who never had walked."

- **14:9-10** "The same heard Paul speak: who steadfastly beholding him, and perceiving that he had faith to be healed, said with a loud voice, 'Stand upright on thy feet, And he leaped and walked.'"

Objection #5 -

You just can't tell God what to do (can't "name it and claim it")

Well, first of all, let me say we are not "telling God what to do" when we "name and claim" what He has promised to give us. We are following God's directions as found in **1 John 5:14-15**. We are asking, according to the revealed will of God.

- **1 John 5:14** "And this is the confidence that we have in him: that if we ask any thing according to his will, he heareth us,

- **5:15** "and if we know that he hears us, whatsoever we ask, we know that we have the petitions that we desired of him."

In **Romans 8:32,** we see that God has already sent Jesus to the cross, giving his very best for the purchase of our full redemption which includes healing. In **1 Peter 2:24**, God put our sicknesses on Jesus for the provision of our bodily healing. This healing is a past tense provision and redemptive right of all God's children. God is telling us to do this. We are not telling God what to do. He tells us to come boldly to the throne of grace and obtain grace to help in time of need. We see Him say this in **Hebrews 4:16**, which is as follows:

- **Hebrews 4:16**: "Let us therefore come boldly unto the throne of grace, that we may obtain mercy, and find help in time of need."

Even though most prayer requests are for help when we have physical needs, we are not to plead and beg to Jesus. His word tells us to "come boldly to the throne." In fact, he says we are to "speak to the mountain" and it shall move, and we "shall have whatsoever we ask."

Objection #6 -

You are denying symptoms and being dishonest and "faking it."

As the father of our faith, Abraham set the standard for a strong faith that gives glory to God. We see this in **Romans 4:17-21:**

- **4:17** "As it is written, I have made thee a father of many nations, before him whom he believed, even God, who quickeneth the dead, and calleth those things which be not as though they were.

- **4:18** Who against hope believed in hope, that he might become the father of many nations, according to that which was spoken, so shall thy seed be.

- **4:19** And being not weak in faith, he considered not his own body now dead, when he was about an hundred years old, neither yet the deadness of Sarah's womb.:

- **4:20** He staggered not at the promise of God through unbelief, but was strong in faith, giving glory to God;

- **4:21** And being fully persuaded that, what he had promised, he was able also to perform."

Even though your symptoms are a fact, the reality of God's sovereign power supersedes all of these natural facts.

It was a natural fact that a 100-year-old man and a 90-year-old woman could not have a baby! However, the word of God said it was already an established fact. By believing the Word of God, this couple simply needed to "catch up with the forever settled word;" we see this in **Psalms 119:89,** "Forever, O Lord, thy word is settled in heaven."

It is our choice what we choose to believe, confess, and live by. What we choose, whether the word of man, our symptoms, circumstances, religious opinions, or the Word of God, will determine our reality. We see this in the following scriptures about confessing what God has promised as reality that supersedes all natural facts:

- **Deuteronomy 30:19** "I call heaven and earth to record this day against you, that I have set before you life and death, blessing and cursing: therefore choose life, that both thou and thy seed may live:"

- **Joel 13:10** "Let the weak say, "I am strong""

- **Matthew 12:34** "Out of the abundance of the heart the mouth speaks."

- **2 Corinthians 4: 13** "We having the same spirit of faith. ...I believed therefore have I spoken."

- **Philippians 2:13** "For it is God who works in you both to will and to do for His good pleasure."

He is working His word in our minds, and working His healing in our bodies for His good pleasure. One good example is in Mrs. Dodie Osteen's miraculous healing from metastatic liver cancer. When people asked her how she felt, she never confessed that she felt bad. She said, "I am blessed of the Lord." So she did not tell a lie about the fact that she often felt really lousy, but confessed the truth of the Word of God instead.

Objection #7 -

Jesus healed because he was the Son of God, and passed it on only to the apostles and prophets who all had special gifts, but they no longer operate today.

This is not the truth. It is man's tradition. The Bible fact is that Christ did all His miracles in the power of the Holy Ghost, and not in His own power as the Second Person of the Blessed Trinity. The same Holy Spirit who healed and worked all of Jesus, Paul, and Peter's miracles is also in us to heal and work miracles.

- **Acts 10:38** Peter said, "How God anointed Jesus of Nazareth with the Holy Ghost and power; who went about doing good, and healing all that were oppressed of the devil; for God was with him."

So you see, Jesus did not do one single healing or miracle during the first 30 years of his life. It was not until the Holy Spirit descended upon him at his baptism, and then after the Holy Spirit led him into the wilderness in order to be tested; we read of this in **Luke 4:14**, where it says, "Jesus returned in the power of the Spirit into Galilee." It was the power of the Spirit that did all of the healing and miracles through Jesus. This was not because he was and is the Son of God. This principle is shown in the following verses:

- **John 5:30** Jesus said, "'I can of my own self do nothing: as I hear, I judge: and my judgment is just; because I seek not mine own will, but the will of the Father, which hath sent me.'"

- **John 14:12-14, verse 12** "Jesus said, 'Verily, verily, I say unto you, He that believeth on me, the works that I do shall he do also; and greater works than these shall he do; because I go unto my Father,

- **14:13** "And whatsoever ye shall ask in my name, that will I do that the Father may be glorified in the Son;"

- **14:14** "If ye shall ask any thing in my name, I will do it.'"

If he had not empowered us to do this, why would he say that we who believe are going to do the same works as Jesus, and ones even greater? God always gives us the power to complete what he commands and promises that we can do!

Paul tells us this in **Romans 15:18-19,** where he says, "'For I will not dare to speak of any of those things, which Christ hath not wrought by me. Through mighty signs and wonders, by the power (**dunamis**) of the Spirit of God.'" Paul's statement plainly states that he did all of the signs and wonders by the power of the Spirit of God, not because he was an apostle! In **Romans 8:26-27,** Paul also says, "'The Spirit also helpeth (**sunantilambanetai,** which means, to take hold against) our infirmities (**astheneiais**)'"; this word is the most common word in the Greek language for **"sickness."**

So, the Holy Spirit takes hold against sickness with us! While it is the work of the Spirit to keep making life in our mortal bodies, He will not do this blessed work unless we, God's saints, do our part, and take hold against our sicknesses together with Him!

In Romans 8:11, Paul says, "'But if the Spirit of Him that raised up Jesus from the dead dwells in you, He that raised up Christ from the dead shall also quicken (**zoopoiesei**; from **zoe**-life and **poieo**-I make) your mortal bodies by his Spirit that dwelleth in you.'" The Spirit makes life in our bodies! This is not a reference to the resurrection, for then the word "**nekros**" which signifies "from the dead" is used. Here "**thnetos**," another "word" for "body," is used, which always speaks of a living body not a dead one.

John Calvin said this concerning **Romans 8:11,** "The quickening of the mortal body here cannot refer to the resurrection of the saints, but must mean a giving of life to their bodies, while here upon earth, through the Spirit."

So, from **Romans 8:11** we know that we have the very same Holy Spirit dwelling in us who raised Christ from the dead, who did all of Christ's miracles, Paul's miracles, and Peter's miracles. It is the work of the Holy Spirit to keep making life in these mortal bodies of ours.

Objection #8 -

Ministering healing went away in the first century, because there are no apostles and prophets today.

In **Ephesians 4:8,11-13**, we see that God has set these apostolic and prophetic offices in the church.

- **4:8** "Wherefore he saith, When he ascended up on high, he led captivity captive, and gave gifts unto men.

- **4:11** And he gave some, apostles; and some, prophets; and some, evangelists; and some, pastors and teachers;

- **4:12** For the perfecting (or "training" or "equipping") of the saints for the work of the ministry, for the edifying of the body of Christ;

- **4:13** Till we all come in the unity of the faith, and of the knowledge of the Son of God, unto a perfect man, unto the measure of the stature of the fullness of Christ:"

So, until God notifies us that he has taken the apostles and prophets out of the church, they are still here!

Objection #9 -

Getting people saved is more important that healing, so let's just concentrate on getting people saved.

I agree 110% that people going to heaven, even before their time because of untimely sickness and disease, is better than if they were perfectly healthy and died without being saved! Now that we have established this fact, let me ask those who hold this view a couple of questions. How many have you led to the Lord in the last twelve months? How many new converts have come to Christ in our churches that do not preach healing, as compared to those who do? If you answered that thousands or tens of thousands have been led to the Lord under your life and ministry, then congratulations! Why? For these are the kinds of results men are getting all over the globe who believe and preach the full gospel and include Divine Healing in their ministry!

In India during 2005, the largest crowd ever to assemble in the history of the church, since Jesus left, came together to hear the Word and to be healed through the ministry of Benny Hinn! As a result, over four million people gathered in three days, with tens of thousands coming to Jesus out of Hindu and Muslim backgrounds, because of the demonstration of God's love for the whole man!

My hope is that if you truly believe that the salvation of a man' s soul is important, you will embrace the ministry of Jesus to save men through healing their entire beings. Jesus spent two thirds of his time healing people, because he knew that the body is where we live and He wants it to be his holy indwelling place, the very temple of the Holy Spirit. **1 Corinthians 6:13, 19-20** says, "Meats for the belly, and the belly for meats: but God shall destroy both it and them. Now the body is not for fornication, but for the Lord; and the Lord for the body. What? Know ye not that your body is the temple of the Holy Ghost which is in you, which ye have of God, and ye are not your own? For ye are bought with a price; therefore glorify God in your body, and in your spirit, which are God's."

Objection #10 -

If Divine Healing is true people would never die then, right?

No, divine healing does not mean that we will never die. The Bible says in **Hebrews 9:27** "And as it is appointed unto men once to die, but after this the judgment:...." However, in spite of the fact that we are not going to live forever in these bodies, this does not mean that we have to be in sickness and disease when we die.

- **Psalms 104:29**, "Thou hidest thy face, they are troubled: thou takest away their breath, they die, and return to their dust."

- **Job 5:26** where we read, "Thou shalt come to thy grave in a full age, like as a shock of corn cometh in his season."

Chapter Eight-
Hang on to Your Faith

—+—

After You Have Prayed

I encourage you to hang on to your faith after praying. Our great Father God is never late, even when what we prayed for appears to have died before our eyes. Days, weeks or even years ago what you prayed for may have died. Let's read the whole passage of **John 11** together for encouragement. See how Jesus wanted Mary and Martha to hang onto their faith, even in life's deepest valley- the death of their brother Lazarus.

- **John 11:1-45**: "Now a certain man was sick, Lazarus, of Bethany, the town of Mary and her sister Martha. (It was Mary which anointed the Lord with ointment, and wiped his feet with her hair, whose brother Lazarus was sick.)

Therefore his sisters sent unto him, saying, 'Lord, behold, he whom thou lovest is sick.'

When Jesus heard that, he said, 'This sickness is not unto death, but for the glory of God, that the Son of God might be glorified thereby.'

Now Jesus loved Martha, and her sister, and Lazarus. When he had heard therefore that he was sick, he abode two days still in the same place where he was. Then after that saith he to disciples, 'Let us go into Judea again.'

The disciples said unto him, 'Master, the Jews of late sought to stone thee; and goest thou thither again?' Jesus answered, 'Are there not twelve hours in the day? If any man walk in the day, he stumbleth not, because he seeth the light of this world. But if a man walk in the night, he stumbleth, because there is no light in him.' These things said he: and after that he saith unto them, 'Our friend Lazarus sleepeth; but I go, that I may awake him out of sleep.'

Then said his disciples, 'Lord, if he sleep, he shall do well.' Howbeit Jesus spoke of his death: but they thought that he had spoken of taking of rest in sleep.

Then said Jesus unto them plainly, 'Lazarus is dead. And I am glad for your sakes that I was not there, to the intent ye may believe; nevertheless, let us go unto him.'

Then said Thomas, which is called Didyrnus, unto his fellow disciples, 'Let us also go, that we may die with him.'

Then when Jesus came, he found that he (Lazarus) had been in the grave four days already. Now Bethany was nigh unto Jerusalem, about fifteen furlongs off: And many of the Jews came to Martha and Mary, to comfort them concerning their brother. Then Martha, as soon as she heard that Jesus was coming, went and met him: but Mary sat in the house.

Then said Martha unto Jesus, 'Lord, if thou hadst been here, my brother had not died. But I know, that even now, whatsoever thou wilt ask of God, God will give *it* thee.'

Jesus saith unto her, 'Thy brother shall rise again.'

Martha saith unto him, 'I know that he shall rise again in the resurrection at the last day.'

Jesus said unto her, 'I am the resurrection, and the life: he that believeth in me, though he were dead, yet shall he live: And whosoever liveth and believeth in me shall never die. Believest thou this?

She saith unto him, 'Yea, Lord: I believe that thou art the Christ, the Son of God, which should come into the world.' And when she had so said, she went her way, and called Mary her sister secretly, saying, 'The Master is come, and calleth for thee.' As soon as she heard she arose quickly, and came unto him. Now Jesus was not yet come into the town, but was in that place where Martha met him. The Jews then which were with her in the house, and comforted her, when they saw Mary, that she rose up hastily and went out, followed her, saying, 'She goeth unto the grave to weep there.'

Then when Mary was come where Jesus was, and saw him, she fell down at his feet, saying unto him, 'Lord, if thou hadst been here, my brother had not died.'

When Jesus therefore saw her weeping, and the Jews also weeping which came with her, he groaned in the spirit, and was troubled, and said, 'Where have ye laid him?'

They said unto him, 'Lord, come and see.' Jesus wept.

Then said the Jews, 'Behold how he loved him! And some of them said, 'Could not this man, which opened the eyes of the blind, have caused that even this man should not have died?'

Jesus, therefore again groaning in himself, cometh to the grave. It was a cave, and a stone lay upon it. Jesus said, 'Take ye away the stone.'

Martha, the sister of him that was dead, saith unto him,' Lord, by this time he stinketh: for he hath been *dead* four days.'

Jesus saith unto her, 'Said I not unto thee, that, if thou wouldest believe, thou shouldest see the glory of God?' Then they took away the stone from the place where the dead was laid. And Jesus lifted up eyes, and said, 'Father, I thank thee that thou hast heard me. And I knew that thou hearest me always: but because of the people which stand by I said *ii*, that they may believe that thou hast sent me.' And when he thus had spoken, he cried with a loud voice, 'Lazarus, come forth.' And he that was dead came forth, bound hand and foot with grave clothes: and his face was bound about with a napkin. Jesus saith unto them, 'Loose him, and let him go.' Then many of the Jews which came to Mary, and had seen the things which Jesus did, believed on him."

In these verses, we find Mary and Martha asking the same thing we have thought or asked at times after we have prayed- "Oh Lord why didn't you come? If you had been here when I prayed, my desire wouldn't have died." Or perhaps we may have pleaded other things, such as:

"Lord, don't You know that bills are due the 15th and 30th of each month?"

"Lord, we want the restoration of our marriage right now."

"Lord, we want this child to come home to Jesus immediately because it's getting problematic and embarrassing!"

What did Jesus say to Mary and Martha when they struggled with the timing of answered prayer? He said, (my paraphrase) "Didn't I tell you if you'd believe, you'd see the resurrection power of the Lord?" They said that they knew of a faith based only on the future. They said that they had faith that one day in the "sweet by and by," of the future Jesus would resurrect their brother. In other words, they had hoped that there would be a future event and, in fact, there will be. However, faith in some future event is not going to bring the answers you need, and the deliverance you are desperately seeking! In essence, Jesus said to Mary, Martha, and now to us today: "Dear child don't you realize that you do not have to wait to be healed? No, no, no! You have the verb tenses wrong. You do not have to wait for the sweet by and by. You can be healed now!" The exact encouraging words of Jesus are as follows:

- **John 11:25** "Jesus said unto her, 'I am the resurrection, and the life: he that believeth in me, though he were dead, yet shall he live:

- **John 11:26** And whosoever liveth and believeth in me shall never die. Believest thou this?'"

The question is: do we believe that Jesus, the Creator God, is never late but always on time? He actually stands outside of time in eternity, shouting a resounding "I AM!" to prayers."

What to do when Your Answer has been in the Grave for Four Days

On His arrival, Jesus had found that Lazarus had already been in the tomb for four days! Let us look back into the story's context, starting with **John 11:25**. We see that Bethany was less than two miles from Jerusalem, and many Jews had come to comfort them in the loss of their brother. When Martha heard that Jesus was coming, she went out to meet Him, but Mary stayed at home. "'Lord,' she said, 'if you had been here my brother would not have died, but I know that even now God will give You whatever You ask.'" Jesus said to her, "'Your brother will rise again.'" Martha answered, "'I know he will, because he will rise again at the resurrection at the last day.'"

Jesus said to her that she had gotten her verb tenses wrong. He reminded her that "I AM"; that He was currently, present tense, standing in their midst as the Resurrection and the Life. Then, He explained to her that whoever currently believes in Me will in truth live even though he dies, saying, "'Whoever lives and believes in me will never die. Do you believe this?'"

Jesus is also asking us this question today. When you pray, are you truly believing and being sure of your hope? Are you certain of the invisible reality, or are you putting an answer out there somewhere in the sweet by and by? Jesus asks you: "Do you believe this?"

In **John 11:27**, Martha said, Sure, Lord, I believe that You are the Christ, the Son of God- He who was to come into the world. After saying this, she went back home to her sister, Mary. He stood at the tomb, in **John 11:38**, and was once more deeply moved. As He came to the tomb, it was a cave with a stone laid across it.

In **John11: 39**, Jesus told the people standing there to take away the stone. Before Jesus raised Lazarus, the stone had to be removed. Likewise, He will raise your situation from the dead. He is standing at the entrance of your home, your work, and your body saying, "Take away the stone." What is the stone we need to remove? Some examples of stones are the stone of unbelief, the stone of bitterness, or the stone of resentment toward people. There are also the stones of men's traditions about prayer, and the stone of broken relationships. Everyone has a unique stone in his or her life, which needs to be removed.

Many praying people would respond as Martha did: "But, Lord...." We all have an excuse about our unbelief. It is part of human nature not to admit unbelief. In **John 11:39**, we read that Martha informed the Lord that, "By this time there is a bad odor, for he has been there four days." Jesus said, "Did I not tell you that if you believed, you would see the glory of God?" They took away what was hindering the power of God.

Today it is our unbelief that creates a stench in the sight of God.

In the following verse, we see that Jesus looked up to heaven and prayed. Focus on the way Jesus prayed:

- **John 11:41** "Then, they took away the stone from the place where the dead was laid. And Jesus lifted up eyes, and said, 'Father, I thank thee that thou hast heard me.'"

When Jesus said, "Father, I thank You that You have heard Me." What tense did Jesus use in His prayer? It is past tense. In fact, He goes on and basically says, "I know you heard me, but the only reason I'm talking now is for those around me to benefit."

- **John 11:42** "And I knew that thou hearest me always: but because of the people which stand by, I said it that they may believe that thou hast sent me."

Again, Jesus was not proclaiming His prayer to convince the Father to raise Lazarus. He already knew that He had the answer. He already knew God had heard Him. He said this prayer so when He raised this man from the dead, everyone would believe. He goes on and prays, believing that the Father has heard Him, and always hears Him. Jesus got one hundred percent of His prayers answered, and did so by the same faith that He expects us to exercise!

You must take off the Grave Clothes to be set free

- **John 11:43** "And when he thus had spoken, he cried with a loud voice, 'Lazarus, come forth.'"

- **John 11:44** "And he that was dead came forth, bound hand and foot with grave clothes: and his face was bound about with a napkin. Jesus saith unto them, 'Loose him, and let him go.'"

Lazarus came out with his hands and feet wrapped with linen and a cloth around his face. Jesus told those around Him to take off the grave clothes that still bound Lazarus, and let him go. There are a lot of people that have been raised from their spiritual death and are in Christ, but still need "to take off their grave clothes."

Once we've come to Christ and He raises us from the dead in the waters of baptism, there are still grave clothes that we have to take off. Our grave clothes may be old teachings of unbelief in the supernatural miracles, healing, deliverance, and resurrection power for victorious Christian living today.

Chapter Nine-
How to Live in Divine Health

---+---

Proverbs 4:20-24 - God's Medicine Bottle

- "My son, attend to my words; incline thine ear
  unto my sayings. Let them not depart from thine
  eyes; keep them in the midst of thine heart. For
  they are life unto those that find them, and health
  to all their flesh."

The verses referenced above have been called "God's
Medicine Bottle," because they bring a vividly clear
prescription. The word "health" can also be translated "medicine." God, our Great Physician, says that his Medicine Bottle,
the Bible, brings "health to all our flesh". If there is health in
all our flesh, then there is no room for sickness and disease.
Yes, this clearly promises that our total physical body will
respond to God's remedy if we carefully take it as directed!
So, let us take a closer look at these powerful verses full
of cure for even the incurable.

Proverbs 4:20 "My son, Attend to my words"

This means more than just reading the Bible. It means making a full commitment that some may think is "extreme," or at least very naïve. It is a decision to "attend" to, or focus on 100%, and to put full confidence in the every word of God in the matter of our healing. If God says in this passage that his words are like medicine, then we should study and follow the directions on the Medicine Bottle, which is the Bible!

Doctors do not promise any benefits from the medicine they prescribe unless it is taken according to the directions. One man of God, Derek Prince, said in his book, God's Medicine Bottle, that in receiving his healing from Jesus he "began to bow my head over the Bible three times every day after meals, because that is how people normally take medicine." He said, "God, you have said that these words of yours will be medicine to all my flesh, and I am taking them as my medicine now, in the name of Jesus." Within a few months, with God's medicine taken in that way, the result God promised was achieved. "I was totally healthy in every area of my body."

The first command in the prescription of God is, "attend to my words." This means that we must give them our undivided attention. Our focus should be full and respectful because of the One who is speaking to us. We should not try to "do our homework while watching the television" when God is the subject matter at hand. With our healing at stake, we should turn off all distracting media. Cut out all of the noise that is competing for our attention, and get alone with our Lord Jesus to take "medicine."

Jesus taught that what we listen to, and how we listen, is a key to our healing. In **Mark 4:24** he said, "Take heed what you hear." And then in **Luke 8:18** he exhorted us to "Take heed how you hear." Therefore, it is very important what we listen to as well how we listen.

Another passage that brings this truth about hearing and healing to the forefront is **Exodus 15:26**. Here the Lord said through Moses,

"If you will diligently heed the voice of the LORD your God and do what is right in his sight, give ear to His commandments, and keep all His statutes, I will put none of the diseases upon you which I have brought upon the Egyptians, For I am the LORD who heals you."

Another way to say this is that the Lord is our Doctor! Notice that the Lord our Doctor gives us promises with conditions for healing our body. The first condition is "If you will diligently heed the voice of the Lord your God." When God says, "diligently listen" it is actually a repetitive verb for emphasis. It could be translated something like this, "If you will listen to the voice of the LORD your God." Like the speakers on a sound system, turn your ears on and listen to God with both the right and the left ear as he speaks to you through your study in the Bible.

As we related in an earlier chapter, Mrs. Dodie Osteen was miraculously healed of metastatic liver cancer over 25 years ago! Yet, to this day, she never leaves her home without reading healing scriptures. She knows them by heart, but she still looks them up and reads them. She knows from past experience that God's Word does not fail, yet she has not stopped taking her medicine!

Proverbs 4:20 "Incline thine ear unto my sayings."

Again, let us review the promise of our Great Doctor in **Exodus 15:26.** We read,

"If thou wilt diligently hearken to the voice of the Lord thy God, and wilt do that which is right in his sight, and wilt give ear to his commandments, and keep all his statutes, I will put none of these diseases upon thee, which I have brought upon the Egyptians: for I am the Lord that healeth thee."

Derek Prince explains that the word "incline" in this passage is Old English for "bend down" or "take it down an incline." Picture yourself physically bending down your ear. How can you bend your ear down without bending your head down first?

Thus, we see a picture of bowing our heads down in the presence of our Lord Jesus in humility. The bottom line is that we must remain teachable while inclining our ears to the word of the Lord. It may come from the most unlikely vessel, and one that you think is not the ideal deliverer of the message. It may come from a little child or someone else we feel is "unqualified" to deliver it. Still, we must receive the medicine at the hands of any one of "God's pharmacists."

In **James 1:19-29,** the Lord's own brother, James, says,

"Wherefore, my beloved brethren, let every man be swift to hear, slow to speak, slow to wrath: Wherefore lay apart all filthiness and superfluity of naughtiness, and receive with meekness the engrafted word, which is able to save your souls." Receive it with meekness and without "naughtiness."

What is this naughtiness spoken of here? Well a naughty child is one who talks back to his parent when he is taught or reprimanded. So could God be saying to us today, "Look when I am teaching you- do not talk back to me with your arguments, prejudices, and preconceptions! Do what I say, and don't be naughty about it." We have all had past teachings that did not line us up with this healing Word of God. When we first heard the healing Word of God, it about knocked us over! Well, it is time to lay that entire tradition aside and receive the engrafted Word without the stiff neck of rebellion. Go ahead and "bend down your ear" to the love of your Lord to heal you today.

Proverbs 4:21 "Let them not depart from thine eyes"

What is the word "them" referring to here? **Verses 20-21** remind us that it is "my words....and my sayings." However, it is crucial to know that this instruction of the Great Doctor is more than just reading the Bible. It is meditating on what you are reading in such a way as to find out how you can personally receive what God is offering you. Not letting the Bible depart from our eyes does not just mean reading it through. Many people read the Bible but never hear God. They don't hear God because their minds are occupied with other things. They are worried about the cares of this life, or fail to really concentrate on the last thing God said. How can the Spirit of Truth lead us to more truth when we have neglected the last nugget of gold He gave us yesterday?

Why is it so crucial to not let the Bible depart from our eyes when it comes to maintaining healing and health? It is because the truth as we see it in **Romans 10:17**.

Romans 10:17, "Faith cometh by hearing and hearing by the word of God."

Right now as you read this, you may be saying, "Yes, but I don't have that kind of faith to get or stay healed." The Good News of God is that "faith cometh!" That means the fact that you are inclining your ear unto the word of God by reading this book is bringing the faith that it takes to get and stay healed. Do not despair, your faith is rising up in your heart. Stay with it and your faith will push out all fear and doubt. It is a process, and God is faithful to the process that He instituted.

Jesus brings the importance of focus in the spiritual realm to us in **Luke 11:34**.

Luke 11:34 , "the light of the body is the eye: therefore when thine eye is single, thy whole body also is full of light; but when thine eye is evil, thy body also is full of darkness."

When our eyes are single in focus, the whole body is full of light. **"Single"** can be translated **"simple"** or **"sincere"**. If we would just take the simple meaning from the plain Word of God in sincere childlike faith, we would experience great results in our health. Some are so "clever and educated" that they explain the true meaning of the healing scripture texts away. In this passage in Luke, our Lord shows us the relationship between our spirit and our body. We are full today of whatever we focused on in the past. As light and darkness can not occupy the same space, so also sickness and health are mutually exclusive!

Malachi 4:2 says, "But unto you that fear my name shall the Sun of righteousness arise with healing in his wings: and ye shall go forth, and grow up as calves of the stall."

As the sun is the source of light in our galaxy, the Son of God is our source of both righteousness and healing. Sin and sickness are products of darkness, but righteousness and healing are products of the Sun of righteousness, with healing in his wings. We read more about the source of healing in **Psalms 107:20** and other Old Testament passages.

Psalms 107:20 "He sent forth his word, and healed them."

- **Exodus 23:25**- "And ye shall serve the Lord your God... and I will take sickness away from the midst of thee."

- **Psalms 105:37**- "He brought them forth also with solver and gold: and there was not one feeble person among their tribes."

According to **Hebrews 8:6**. the New Testament is even a better covenant than the Old Testament and is established upon better promises than even these we have looked at above. That is why we can be confident that if God did this for Israel of old, how much more will he do for you in a blood covenant with his very own Son our Lord Jesus!

In giving us the New Testament, God sent the living Word to both validate and guarantee that covenant. He saves and heals us by sending us the Word, our Lord Jesus, who became flesh! **(See John 1:14)** Now, as the body of Christ we all may "lay hands on the sick," as seen in **Mark 16:15-18.** Today our hands are the healing wings of the Son of Righteousness!

We have the very same Holy Spirit dwelling in us who raised Christ from the dead, who did all of Christ's miracles, Paul's miracles, and Peter's miracles. It is the work of the Holy Spirit to keep making life in these mortal bodies of ours.

Proverbs 4:21 "Keep them in the midst of thine heart."

When we keep the words and sayings of God in our heart. we are in a spiritual battle. We must actively fight the good fight of faith using the Word of God, which comes out of our heart through the confession of our mouth. When Jesus said in **Revelation 3:11,**

"Look, I am coming quickly, Hold on to what you have, so that no one will take away your crown," he was making it clear, both to the church of Philadelphia and to us today, that we can lose what we once had."

As this relates to the healing of our body, when symptoms come back or we feel pain again, we must rise up and meet this attack with the Word of God. Command the devil's lying symptoms to be broken in Jesus mighty name! Do not yield to the pain. By using the foundation of the Word of God on healing for ourselves, we can succeed in maintaining health. Jesus taught the following great foundational truth in **Matthew 7:24-29:** "Anyone who listens to my teaching and obeys me is wise, like a person who builds a house on solid rock. Though the rains come in torrents and the floodwaters rise and the winds beat against that house, it won't collapse, because it is built on rock. But anyone who hears my teaching and ignores it is foolish, like a person who builds a house on sand. When the rains and floods and winds beat against that house, it will fall with a mighty crash. After Jesus finished speaking, the crowds were amazed at his teaching, for he taught as one who had real authority-quite unlike the teachers of religious law."

Nahum 1:9 "Affliction will not rise up a second time."

We must stand on His promises and make up our mind that we refuse to accept the illness back on our body! I like what Kenneth E. Hagin said in his message entitled, "**Healing; How to Keep It**." He states, "When you know this in your heart, your spirit your inner man, like you know in your head that 2 +2 is 4, then the devil and his symptoms will have no power over you! That will be the end of them. Know and use the power and the authority of the name of Jesus and you have a Bible right to that name. When symptoms come, you will stand against them in faith and have no doubts or fears. Again, we must make up our mind that we refuse to accept the illness back on our body! Tell the devil that he was whipped by Jesus at the cross. Tell him to leave you now." By submitting ourselves to God and resisting the devil, he will flee, as promised in **James 4:7-8**. We must speak specifically to the symptoms and treat them as enemies. Then, we continue to take God's remedy. This is not a one time shot. On the contrary, taking God's medicine involves daily deciding to actively fight the good fight of faith, and using the Word of God in confession of our healing, coming out of our heart through our mouth. Giving testimony of our healing to others around us, as seen in **Revelation 12:11**, is a crucial way to overcome the enemy.

Finally, put on all the Armor of God as found in **Ephesians 6:10-18**. We must rebuke all our fears, for God has not given us the spirit of fear, but of power, love, and a sound or disciplined mind. We see this in **2 Timothy 1:7**.

Since the heart is the place from where all the medicine is being sent out into the entire body, it is very important that we cast down all thoughts and imaginations that don't line up with the Word of God on healing. We can see how to do this in **2 Corinthians 10:4-5**.

In conclusion, take confidence that as God says in **Philippians 2:13,**

"It is God who works in you both to will and to do for His good pleasure."

My friends, believe that even as you have read this book, it is God who is working His word in your mind and working His healing in your body for His good pleasure!

Bibliography

Aterburn, Stephen. Stoeker, Fred. Yorkey, Mike. Every Man's Battle. Colorado Springs: WaterBrook Press, 2000.

Avanzini, Dr. John F. Paul's Thorn: "Satan's Messenger, Not Sickness.". John F. Avanzini, 1980.

The Bantam Medical Dictionary. Bantam Books, 1981.

Bosworth, F. F. Christ The Healer. Grand Rapids: Chosen, 1924.

Copeland, Gloria. And Jesus Healed Them All. Fort Worth: Kenneth Copeland Publications, 1981.

Copeland, Kenneth. Healing: it is Always God's Will. Fort Worth: Kenneth Copeland Publications, 1983.

Hagin Jr., Kenneth E. Healing and How to Keep It. RHEMA Bible Church, 1989.

Kuhlman, Kathryn. Healing Words. Lake Mary: Charisma House, 1997.

Kenyon, E.W. Jesus the Healer. Kenyon's Gospel Publishing Society, 2004.

McCrossan, Dr. T. J. Bodily Healing and The Atonement. RHEMA Bible Church, 1982.

Osteen, Dodie. Healed of Cancer. Nashville: Thomas Nelson Publishers, 2003.

Pettys, Gregory S. Prayers God Loves to Answer. ASPIRE GROUP, INC, 2005.

Prince, Derek. God's Medicine Bottle. New Kensington: Whitaker House Publishers, 1984.

Roberts, Oral. God Still Heals Today: And Here's How He Heals You. Oral Roberts, 1984.

Sumrall, Lester. Miracles Don't Just Happen. South Bend: LeSEA Publications, 1979.

Webster. Library of Practical Information. Lexicon Publishers, Inc., 1986.

About the Editors

—+—

- **Evelyn Schumacher** - Evelyn Schumacher lives in Springfield, Illinois with her feline friend, Lady. She works for a local chiropractor. She has two sons, Rod Schumacher and Curt Schumacher. Rod is in international sales with Thomas Nelson Publishers; he lives in Nashville, Tennessee, with his wife Brenda and their two boys, Justin and Braden. Curt is an elementary school principal in Edwardsville, Illinois, where he and his wife Beth live with their two girls, Sarah and Kylie. Evelyn's grandchildren are the light of her life.

- **Alicia Pettys** - Alicia Pettys is the daughter of the author of this book. She is fourteen years old, and will be a sophomore at Springfield High School in Springfield, IL in 2006-2007; there she is an honor student involved with Student Council, the school newspaper, and various clubs. She also plays varsity basketball for her school, and it is her main extracurricular activity. At home, Alicia loves to play with her brothers, and tries to do all she can to help her mother. She aspires to make a career in either journalism; advertising; or public administration, which involves social justice in the areas of government, ethics, and international law.

CPSIA information can be obtained
at www.ICGtesting.com
Printed in the USA
LVHW09s2141181018
594096LV00001B/35/P

9 781600 346163